Contemporary Commonwealth Literature

Contemporary Commonwealth Literature

edited by

R.K. DHAWAN

Prestige Books

Published by
Prestige Books
3/28, East Patel Nagar
New Delhi 110 008
Mobile: 9818755529

ISBN: 81-7551-177-X

Printed at Chaman Offset Press, New Delhi 110 002

Contents

Commonwealth Literature: Current Scene

R.K. DHAWAN
S.B.S. College, University of Delhi

The last few years have registered a rich growth of literary works by Indian writers. The most significant contribution in this regard has been made by the writers of Indian Diaspora. Migration has played an important role in the cultural scenario of countries like America, Canada, England and Australia. Multiculturalism is an ideology that appreciates the value of diversity—of culture, languages and religions. The policy of multiculturalism has given rise to a considerable body of fiction written by immigrant writers. Foreign lands have given Indians fame and success; their bond with the country of their origin is strongly embedded in their writings. A few popular novels are being made into films. Noted immigrant director Mira Nair will be filming two new diasporic novels: Jhumpa Lahiri's *The Namesake* and Hari Kunzru's *The Impressionist*. Writers like Vikram Seth, Rohinton Mistry, Anita Desai, Bharati Mukherjee, Sujata Bhat, Amitav Ghosh, Shauna Singh Baldwin, Anita Rau Badami and Rahul Varma have recently brought out new works. The diasporic fiction is a story of those who maintained the culture they left behind. And at the same time, they became an important part of their adopted countries. Many of these writers have received international acclaim. Most significant releases this year were: Rushdie's *Shalimar the Clown*, Vikram Seth's *Two Lives* and Bharati Mukherjee's *The Bride*.

At home front, there is a phenomenal growth of Indian writing in English. Interestingly, India has emerged as a huge market for self-help books. There is now a great demand for inspirational books. The business of motivation is on a roll these days, with a plethora of inspirational books jostling for shelf space in libraries and bookshops. The spiritual gurus are giving mantras, telling us how to manage our life. Books by authors like Deepak Chopra, Shiv Khera and Arindam Chaudhuri have taken the market by storm. This new-emerging area has given a great fillip to Indian writing in English.

It is Indian English fiction, however, which is growing from strength to strength. There is a new group of writers who are making waves in the literary circles, forcing readers to see beyond the traditional writers. Names like Anurag Mathur, Navtej Sarna, Namita Gokhale, Ruchir Joshi, Manju Kapur, Kalyan Roy, Pankaj Mishra and Kamal Jha have become so well known as they are bringing great laurels to the realm of Indian writing in English. *Q and A*, a debut novel by Vikas Swarup, has created ripples in the literary world. The author, a diplomat in External Affairs Ministry, has sold this novel in over fifteen countries and even won a film contract. It is a book for everyone. What's so wonderful about Swarup is that he has a sense of humour, a great imagination and subtle artistry. Kalyan Roy, a Calcutta scholar who teaches in the States, has just published his novel *Eastwards*. The novel is crowded with mythical and Shakespearean characters, replete with literary allusions in a comparative framework.

Going by the abundance of new books on Indian themes, one wonders why our authors feel compelled to present their country's exotica in order to ensure wide readership, especially in the West. Many writers from South Asia, like Chandani Lokuge from Sri Lanka, Adib Khan from Bangladesh and Amitav Ghosh from India have depicted their countries in 'romantic' fashion, the way Europeans imagine this part of the world. India, for example, has often been projected as a land of palaces, remote hills, peacocks and elephants. The latest in this genre is the highly-praised novel of Amitav Ghosh entitled *The Hungry Tide* which calls for a brief discussion here. The novel offers us the history of Sunderbans region, the precarious ecology of the river dolphins and the great Bengal tigers living there. Here, at the beginning of the last century, a visionary Scotsman founded a utopian settlement where peoples of all races, classes and religions could live together. Ghosh interlaces a plethora of details—scientific, ecological, and cultural—into the story. He produces, in the process, a rich specimen of exotica. Unlike his other novels, *The Hungry Tide* has few characters and covers the events of just a month. An anthropologist by profession, Ghosh makes a serious investigation into the subject of the theme of the novel.

Ghosh sets *The Hungry Tide* in the Sunderbans islands lying below Calcutta on the gulf between India and Bangladesh. Sunderbans islands are located in the Bay of Bengal, sort of an extension of Bengal. We have here Bengali villagers who eke out their living in the mangroves and mud, and are in constant fear of being eaten up by crocodiles and tigers. It is a setting where everyone is on an equal footing. The settlers of the Sunderbans believe that anyone without a pure heart who ventures into the weary labyrinth will never return.

The story begins at a railway station at the entrance to the Sunderbans, with the incidental meeting between the two main characters, Kanai Dutt, a sophisticated businessman, and Piyali Roy, an American scientist who has come to study the rare dolphin which lives in the rivers of the tide country. Piya hires an illiterate boatman Fokir to guide her through the backwaters in her search for the dolphin. She unravels the mystery concerning the dolphins which are said to live in the local waters. Piya does not share common language, but she shares with Kanai and Fokir the quest for knowledge. The story is told from the perspective of Piya and Kanai, the two main characters.

Kanai Dutt, educated as translator and owner of a successful translation business, comes to the island of Lusibari to visit his aunt, Nilima. He has come to the islands on the request of his aunt, a local figure, for the first time since the death of his uncle, a political radical. He had been to Lusibari as a teenager, sent by his parents to be exiled for his pride and arrogance. He has been now summoned by Nilima because of a package left to Kanai by her husband, Nirmal, which has been found some twenty years after his death.

Piyali Roy is the daughter of Bangla parents who had immigrated to Seattle. She is a woman used to the solitude and rigours of the life of a scientist working in the field. She often works in areas where she knows neither the customs nor the language; she can survive for days just on dry foodstuff. She has come to the Sunderbans to find these rare creatures and alien culture.

With the writing of this new novel, Ghosh has discovered another new territory, a fascinating place, another world, a kind of exotica emerging from history and myth of the place. Epical in scope, the novel has captured readers' imagination the world over.

While celebrating the publications of new works that have enriched the global literary corpus this year, there is a tinge of sadness, nevertheless. This is so as a number of noted literary figures passed away recently. We earnestly pay our tributes to them. These include Mulk Raj Anand, the father of Indian English novel; Kamala Markandaya, a pioneering woman novelist; Shama Futehally, a young novelist of *Tara Lane* fame; and eminent poets Nissim Ezekiel, Dom Moraes, Arun Kolatkar and Amrita Pritam. Also passed away Saul Bellow, the eminent Jewish-American writer, and Jacques Derrida, perhaps the best known literary critic in the world who contributed to the evolution of critical theory in the modern times, and Susan Sontag, an American writer and philosopher of culture, who wrote best-selling novels like *The Volcano Lover* and *In America*. The deaths of these writers have created a vacuum that will not be filled for many years to come.

The Pitfalls of Magic Realism and the Fall from Paradise: The Rape of Kashmir in Salman Rushdie's *Shalimar the Clown*

DAVID MYERS
University of Queensland

The dramatic yarn of Salman Rushdie's new novel *Shalimar the Clown* is spun out in three tragic strands. The novel is an extremely ambitious work in which the personal, the political and the ideological are intertwined to create a powerful, but flawed, masterpiece. Rushdie is a brilliant storyteller but perhaps too much the self-conscious postmodernist showman with a full bag of magic tricks. Nevertheless, his grim evocation of poor, doomed Kashmir is an act of big-hearted courage; it is at times deeply moving and at times shattering in its horror. His politicization of the novel demonstrates his commitment to the cause of inter-cultural, inter-racial tolerance and serves to augment rather than detract from a Romeo and Juliet love story with a perverse twist.

The first of his three narrative strands deals with the ill-fated personal lives of his three main characters: Boonyi, the beautiful, sensual young Hindu dancer; Shalimar Noman a handsome young Muslim tightrope walker and clown who is her lover and husband; and the ruthless old philanderer, Jewish European Max Ophuls, who destroys their sacred marriage. When young love is blighted, Shalimar, harmless, tender Shalimar the clown, gifted artist of almost mystic balance, is horrifyingly transformed into Shalimar the assassin and savage avenger.

The second narrative strand is the tale of two Kashmiri villages, Pachigam and Shirmal, which suffer the fall from paradise to the inferno of hell. Pachigam was famous for its traditional entertainments and dance performances of ancient myths and known for the sensible and humorous co-existence of its mixed Hindu and Muslim population. Shirmal was a friendly rival village of Muslims, known for its traditional cooking art and the serving of its festival dinners of "minimum 36 courses." Together the two villages represent a paradise of innocence, peace and common-sense tolerance. They are located in the fragrance and fertility of Kashmir, a hidden Shangri-la or Garden of Eden. Their fall is caused by the intrusion from outside of religious bigotry, ideological arrogance and militaristic fundamentalism.

The third narrative strand is a documentary survey of Kashmiri history from the Partition of 1949, but more particularly from the first India-Pakistan war of 1965 through to the bloody insurgencies of the following decades and the military impasse that continues to this present day. This period covers the drawing up of the Line of Control and the emergence of the insurgent movement, 'Kashmir for the Kashmiris' and the guerilla incursions of Islamist militants trained in the mountains on the Pakistani border. It also covers the increasing belligerence and brutality of the Indian army of occupation parallelled by the savage depredations of a Pakistan-supported guerilla army of Islamist fundamentalists and, ultimately, fidayeen suicide bombers.

This is not a novel for the faint-hearted and the author pulls no punches. His own family roots lie with his beloved grandparents in Kashmir and there is no doubt that he feels the tragic mutilation of the region all the more bitterly. This is a very serious work—though not lacking at the individual level in farce and comic relief—and Rushdie is at pains to show even-handedly the irreparable evil that has been done by both sides. While the focus of the world news has been on the wars in Palestine, Afghanistan and Iraq, the rape of Kashmir has been largely overlooked as a mere sideshow by the western media. But the intensity of the destruction of a whole culture and the 320,000 Hindu pandits driven into refugee camps in exile have been no less real for all that. The novelist uses all his art and all three narrative strands to show how, step-by-step, narrow-mindedness and dogma become murderous self-righteousness and fanaticism. As he says in the novel *Shalimar the Clown's* epitaph in a quotation from Shakespeare's *Romeo and Juliet*, 'a plague on both your houses.'

It is now a decade and a half since 1989 when the fatwah was imposed on Rushdie by the Ayatollah Khomeini of Iran because of the novel *The Satanic Verses*. Now in 2005 with *Shalimar the Clown* Rushdie seems set to re-ignite the old controversy. True, this time there is no questioning in the novel of the divine origins of the sacred Koran. And true, Rushdie is very even-handed in his condemnation of both the Indian army of occupation and the Pakistani guerrillas. His indictment of alleged atrocities by the Indian army of occupation under the euphemism of "crackdown" is truly horrifying. Equally, however, his scornful depiction of the fire and brimstone sermons of the Iron Mullahs and their terrorist training camps in the high mountains separating Pakistan and Kashmir will win him no friends among righteous Islamists. His recent call on worldwide television for Islamists to modernize the Islamic faith was undoubtedly courageous, though perhaps not wise. His evocation in this novel of how Shalimar the clown becomes Shalimar the assassin is at times flawed by melodramatic overwrite or by tasteless farce and sheer verbiage, but the novel is nevertheless an extraordinarily powerful revelation about the perversion of innocence and the brave but futile attempt by Boonyi and one or two other Kashmiri women to find redemption.

On the personal level, when you think about it, *Shalimar the Clown* is not at all a love story that goes wrong. On the contrary. It is a story of terror, a killer-thriller. In the beginning Rushdie leads us astray with a beautiful evocation of Boonyi's virginal romance in the midnight meadows of Khelmarg. But from then onwards, it is all hatred and terror. Even the new "love," for the sake of which Boonyi foolishly abandons her husband, is not love at all. It turns out very quickly to be crass, mutual exploitation, she of his money and power, and he of her body. Quickly even these shallow pleasures turn to ashes and they are transformed through disillusionment to despair and mutual hatred. Boonyi's foolish and naïve resolve to turn her back on her first love out of lust for the false glamour and consumerism of the city turns out to be a fatal miscalculation. She never gets a second chance.

In other relationships in the novel, the "Rat's" clumsy love for ambassador Max Ophuls slowly sours into hatred and divorce. In return, Max comes to hate her for her poor parenting of India (Kashmira), his illegitimate daughter whom she wickedly stole from the biological mother Boonyi. This child, called India Ophuls, hates her foster-mother as a teenager and tries out drugs and prostitution in her despair. (Rushdie's narratives swing madly from one extreme to another.) Admittedly, when Kashmira is rescued by her father Max, she does in return love him, but this doesn't stop her from being largely incapable of womanly erotic love for any man. Instead, she trains fanatically at archery, shooting, boxing and martial arts. She even tells the poetic Kashmiri gentleman who woos her that in their relationship he is the female and she is the male. This lady is seriously kinky. Her life is not inspired by love, but by rage and hatred. When she finally discovers, much later, how Shalimar murdered her mother, she re-names herself Kashmira Noman and dedicates her life to hatred of Shalimar who murdered both her mother and her father. When Shalimar rots in prison awaiting trial for the murder of her father Max, she writes him hundreds of poisonous hate-letters. And when Shalimar miraculously escapes from Death Row in San Quentin prison, she doesn't hide in maidenly terror. On the contrary. Like the classical goddess of the hunt, Diana, she takes out her bow and arrows and becomes the huntress lusting to take revenge by hunting him down. There is simply no room for love or forgiveness or understanding in this woman.

And as for Shalimar himself, even at the very moment of consummating his love for fourteen-year-old virginal Boonyi, he swears solemnly that if she is ever unfaithful, he will kill her, her lover and their child if there is one. The structure of the whole novel is based on this all-consuming hatred. When he is taught fundamentalism and puritanism in the terrorist-training camps along the high mountain borders with Pakistan, he quickly becomes a maniacal assassin. He actually enjoys killing. Apart from his political assassinations, he murders his wife by cutting off her head. Years later, with no less brimstone in his belly, he slits the throat of her lover, Max. And still not sated, he then comes to kill Kashmira. So, this is most definitely not a love novel, it is a killer-thriller. Shalimar's mind is hopelessly poisoned by personal hatred and ideological propaganda. He never feels the slightest nostalgia for past bliss, doubt in his murderous mission, or remorse. For a whole lifetime he is nothing more than a killing machine.

Similarly, it is not life that stimulates Rushdie's greatest writing gifts, but violent death (318). The most powerful scenes in the novel are those that witness the humiliation, murder, rape and destruction of the village of Pachigam, and the destruction of the friendly rival village Shirmal. This is so because Rushdie has consistently evoked a pre-crisis bucolic idyll in rural Kashmir in these two villages, and he has combined this nostalgia with ominous prophecies of the veil that is to come, especially as spoken by the forest witch, N. The idyll before the storm is constructed from the fertility and the beauty of the Kashmiri fields and gardens, the saffron fields, the chinar trees, the glory days of Mughal rule or even Sikh rule, and evocations of the fabled gardens of Shalimar by Lake Dall just outside Srinagar.

There is a human dimension to this pre-crisis idyll. That is, the inhabitants of the two rival villages, Pachigam and Shirmal, solve their disagreements with humour, moderation and intercultural common sense compromise. They bend ideologies and dogmas to suit their friendship. This is how the Hindu-Islamic wedding of Boonyi and Shalimar is celebrated—with tolerance, humour and a spirit of give and take, live and let live.

This idyll of tolerance contrasts sharply with the extraordinary heartlessness of the main characters. They all seem quite incapable of the humour, friendship and forgiveness needed to live a life of moderation and moderate happiness. Enough for them is never enough. They always want more. Boonyi very selfishly and without a moment's thought on the misery she will cause, wants more glamour, adventure and city life. Max Ophuls wants more glamour, more power, more prestige and more sexual adventures. Shalimar wants to kill, again and again.

Worse, no one knows how to forgive, or to forgive and forget. The main characters seem driven and possessed by the demons of hate and monomaniacal revenge. There is no question of Shalimar ever forgiving Boonyi. He never has a second's doubt in his insane compulsion to murder her. But Boonyi never forgives herself either. Her decade or two of living in utter solitude, in ostracism from her beloved village, being declared "a dead person," the penance she gladly imposes upon herself, none of it is enough. The villagers do not forgive her and she does not forgive herself. She bares her throat willingly, almost in relief, to her husband-assassin's knife. For another decade Shalimar mindlessly pursues her adulterous partner Max Ophuls and also his illegitimate daughter Kashmira. He never has a second's doubt. There are no complex emotions within him. But he is not the only one. Boonyi's daughter Kashmira is a highly unfeminine parallel. Single-mindedly she trains daily with her bow and arrows, guns and martial arts. Obsessively she writes hundreds of letters of murderous hatred to Shalimar the assassin in prison. She loves, not for the sake of future love or art. She lives for one purpose only: to kill Shalimar. Is there all that much to choose between the two of them? Are they not both equally perverted?

II

Salman Rushdie's favoured narrative mood in the opening section of this saga is the affectation of world-weary sage, shaking his head now in Olympian amazement and now in sorrow at human fanaticism, perversions and hatreds. His favourite narrative technique is to marry the grotesque and the farcical in the background, and then, at his best, to superimpose a tender and affectionate tale in the foreground. Unfortunately, however, there are leakages between background and foreground and at his worst the foreground plot about the main characters sometimes becomes swamped in lurid hyperbole and farce.

Rushdie is perhaps most relaxed with his backgrounds and minor characters because there he can let loose his penchant for caricature and the absurd. He has a Russian potato-mystic in L.A. casting aspersions on all "guys" (she is trying to say "gays") and he has a beautiful Kashmiri woman also in L.A. trying to remember whether the "super-averagely attractive . . . and goofy" male model who has just proposed marriage to her is named Jock Flock or Rick Flick. In these background sketches realism doesn't even get a look in. His parody of another minor character, a cockney woman-cleaner in London, is an outrageous travesty of Charles Dickens's phoneticisation of a Cockney's mispronunciations.

With the main characters Rushdie likes to bring in a mythical framework wherever possible. The novel's heroine, who subsequently becomes the novel's anti-heroine in a bewildering volte-face by Rushdie, starts out as a gorgeous, sensual virgin village girl in remote Kashmir. She is swiftly clad in Hindu myth. She is not just her cheeky self, plotting her secret erotic rendezvous at midnight, she is also Sita Devi being magically "abducted" by Ravan the demon king in the *Ramayana*. Rushdie cannot resist bringing in mythical allusion and alleged classical parallels.

Rushdie's favourite narrative technique is to stand astride the globe, remote, perhaps even from a satellite in orbit, giving a glimpse of Gorbachev here, a moment in a famous South African prison there, insert a scandalous anecdote about the Prince of Wales urinating, indulge in a highly improbable erotic scene between an 80 year old ex-ambassador and a famous young Indian starlet, and then speculate about the underground Lizard People of the Los Angeles sewers. Into this curious global garbage bag of unrelated tit bits, he suddenly throws a garish murder on centrestage, and bingo, his main plot has begun at the end with the murder of ageing roué Max Ophuls by the outraged Kashmiri husband, Shalimar the Clown, who has nursed his wrath and his implacable revenge for some twenty years.

At his best Rushdie is a master storyteller. He entrances the reader with the romance and the spine-chilling menace of a story. When temporary heroine, Hindu girl Boonyi resolves to give her virginity to Muslim boy Noman Shalimar Noman he has thousands of details to give the scene both local colour and also mythic resonance. Boonyi smokes charas to give herself courage and walks to the midnight tryst bearing a little pot of hot coals below her belly (60). Mythically, she is compared with Sita. Shalimar brings with him the sky-dragons of his father, Rahu and Ketu, and also the snake-witchcraft of his mother Firdaus Begum (56). There is a magic in Shalimar's clownish tight rope walking, but his promise out of enthralled love to walk on air and if she should ever be unfaithful to him to murder her cast a chilling shadow over their first love-making. It is this promise which gives narrative tension to the whole novel, even though we know how he murders ex-ambassador Max Ophuls right at the beginning of the work. The question is how does he come to do this deed and why does it take him some twenty years.

In his arch-romantic evocation of the paradise of Kashmir and the Mughal Shalimar Gardens, Rushdie draws heavily on folk legend, superstition—a prophetic witch in the forest, the harmonious co-existence of Hindus and Muslims and their religious rituals in village life—and inter-village rivalry in the festivals called the dinners of "the Thirty Six Courses Minimum." It is an irresistibly colourful mélange of daily provincial life rendered with great expertise. This is the golden age of Kashmir before the beginning of the India-Pakistan war in 1965 and before the advent of the so-called iron mullahs who preach fanaticism and intolerance to their congregations. Paradise is about to be destroyed by sectarian hatred and war and Rushdie depicts this shameful fall from paradise movingly, even tragically, in the first half of his novel.

The beginning of the end occurs at a grand folk festival in the Shalimar Gardens. The festival is ruined by the freezing snowfall and by the panicky rumours that a murderous guerilla army is invading from Pakistan. Two babies are born during this festival and one mother dies in childbirth. The two babies are Boonyi and Shalimar. For fourteen more years the rift between the two remote villages is plastered over and a semblance of peace and harmony prevails. But then adventurous, bold Boonyi gives herself to Shalimar and insists on marrying him. What should have been a guarantee of the harmony to come is instead the excuse given to envious zealots to destroy the inter-racial and inter-religious harmony of the region. "The time of demons had begun." (88)

In *Shalimar the Clown* Rushdie constructs the myth of a golden age of inter-religious and inter-racial harmony. This golden age is located in the fabled valley of Kashmir. Chronologically it may be located at the power peak of the Mughal Empire in the 16th century, or again at the time of the Sikh emperors in the 18th century. But paradoxically, the golden age reaches its peak not in the palaces of the powerful, but in the humble Kashmiri villages of Pachigam and Shirpal, two villages which engage in friendly rivalry but which never descend to the barbarity of hatred and war, even though Pachigam is co-inhabited by Hindu pandits and the Muslims led by Sarpanch Abdullah Noman. In a landscape sense this golden age is comprised of the fertility of the fields with their rich saffron crops and the wildflowers of the mountain meadows of Khelmarg and the celestial chinar tree after which the heroine Boonyi names herself. The distinctive human feature of the Kashmiri villagers' golden age is the humorous, broad-minded subversion of all ideology and rigid dogma. Dogma is bent by the villagers until it can accommodate the needs of 'the other.' Tolerance of 'the other' and friendly compromise achieve their highest ethical moment in the wedding ceremony of the Hindu girl Boonyi and the Muslim boy Shalimar Noman. Each religion conducts its tradition rituals and both sides are happy (apart from a few bad-tempered mutterings by die-hard dogmatists who are quickly overruled). This golden age is destroyed by the vanity, selfishness and frivolity of Boonyi and then subsequently by the vow of ruthless vengeance taken by Shalimar the puritan. The spirit of an outraged religious law on monogamy is avenged without a single thought of the possibility of forgiveness or compassion.

Even though Salman Rushdie the narrator is apparently a rationalist, this in no way impedes the flow of the usual narrative devices of magic realism. *Shalimar the Clown* is full of jokey references to myths and superstitions, loads of omens and prophecies and flirtations with the supernatural. There are the repeated prophecies of the earth witch of the forest Nazarebaddoor with her 'evil eye, begone' (63), the superstitious legend of the two dragon planets Rahu and Ketu (45-47), the legend of the gold-digging ants (74), the miracle of the Seventh Sarkar, who can make the Shalimar Gardens disappear (77), the magic snake-totemism of Firdaus Noman ("Snake wriggle, world jiggle" [56]) and so on. There is an ambivalent, bantering filter through which these references to the supernatural are passed, so that author and reader enjoy the best of both worlds: the superstitious shiver at the supernatural and the amused distance of the rationalist.

Certainly there is no point in approaching Salman Rushdie's narrative art by the criteria of say psychological realism. You will search in vain for detailed character motivation and carefully prepared historical or environmental backgrounds. Instead Rushdie breezily substitutes the techniques of magic realism—a potent brew of hints of the supernatural, lots of folk superstitions and latherings of Hindu and classical Greek polytheistic myths. Against this jokey backdrop Rushdie pits the wilful and sometimes sinful outbursts of the individual breaking free of the rigid traditions of the local community. This is in particular the fate of Boonyi. The novel begins with a playful tone and rushes erratically along towards the horror of the climax and catastrophe and then reverts to the macabre playfulness of the novel's open ending.

So, for example, when Rushdie is confronted with the task of rendering Shalimar the Clown's miraculous escape from maximum security San Quentin prison, he simply skips the boring realistic detail of how this was possible. Instead he reverts to the youthful nature-mysticism of Shalimar's tight rope walking in which the rope somehow becomes only a thickened substantiation of the air. He flies, or glides or whatever and mere mortals are astounded. All courtesy of magic realism. Similarly, like a supernatural ninja assassin, Shalimar breaks through the sophisticated electronic detectors of Kashmira's burglar alarms because he has the mysterious sixth sense. Shalimar's hideous metamorphosis from mystic clown-artist of the tight rope to brainwashed zombie and Manchurian candidate assassin is no doubt fabulous entertainment, but it is totally lacking in emotional complexity, in self-doubt or remorse. Shalimar is become a one-dimensional assassin, full stop.

The decisive actions of the main characters are intertwined with playfully suggested mythical archetypes. Of course these heroic myths are deliberately and humorously at variance with the more selfish and less dignified motivations of the novel's earthly characters and that is all part of the fun.

The folk superstitions, apart from providing bags of wonderful, exotic local colour, are used as omens and portents of the horrors to come. For the movement of the novel is inexorably away from a tongue-in-cheek golden age of inter-racial harmony and downwards to the tragic and horrific anarchy of terrorism and the destruction of all hope and confidence. The bad omens and the dire prophecies of the village witches are like classical Greek choruses in predicting and commenting on the tragic inevitability of the coming catastrophe. It seems to take only the foolish vanity of Boonyi in wanting the glamour of the cosmopolitan world, or the equally foolish and compulsive womanizing of ambassador Max Ophuls to bring about a tragedy of murderous violence and herald the destruction of the delicate fabric of the whole of Kashmiri society. But of course this is only the personal moral fable. Historically, Islam, characterized by intolerant puritanism and fundamentalism meet the West, marked by laissez-faire licentiousness and individual self-indulgence. The tragic explosion that follows this clash is inevitable.

The fall from paradise begins when three oafish Muslim boys act stupidly and brutally after the fire-breathing sermons of a sulphurous iron mullah in their local mosque. They capture an innocent Hindu girl from the neighbouring village while she is gathering flowers and rape her. The girl's father, a stalwart man, swears revenge. Fully armed, he gallops his mountain pony to the Muslim village where the three guilty rapists flee into the sanctuary of the mosque. Even though there are three of them and only one of him, they are too cowardly to come out and face a father's retribution. They cower inside and starve to death. The mosque is padlocked and never again used. This is a spine-chilling story and Rushdie tells it well. It reminds one of Igmar Bergman's *Virgin Spring.* The immediate, hot-blooded vengeance of the brave father is of course meant to act as a strange contrast to the initial failure of Shalimar the Clown to react when his bride becomes the shamefully kept woman of the American ambassador to India, Max Ophuls. The contrast is the more compelling because Boondie knows that it is her provocative marriage with Muslim Shalimar Noman that is the real cause of Muslim rage and the rape committed by the three stupid boys. It is her inter-religious adventurousness which has provided the excuse for the fanatics to destroy the paradise of Kashmir. Rushdie is skilful at such parallels and narrative linkages.

If *Shalimar the Clown* is to succeed as a novel—a novel about persuasive individual human beings as opposed to a humanist, political essay on religious zealotry—Rushdie has to persuade us of the tragic inevitability of teenage Boonyi's sexual relationship with the ageing American-Jewish Max Ophuls in Delhi. He has to make the encounter crackle with drama and the insanity of whirlwind passion. The question is whether he can achieve this liaison without blackening both their characters? The answer is that he cannot and indeed he doesn't even try.

In fact there is an unhealable rift in *Shalimar the Clown* between the Kashmiri scenes of the young Boonyi and the crass, adulterous scenes years later in Delhi. In Delhi the Jewish hero, Max Ophuls, becomes the leering anti-hero. Boonyi's earlier sexual awakening in Kashmir produced scenes which were tender, evocative, humorous, richly embroidered and ultimately tragic. But the scenes given to the adultery with Max Ophuls in Delhi are vulgar, exaggerated, ugly and farcical. It is almost as though Rushdie ran out of interest in his own creation, and having become impatient with both the plot and the main characters he begins to lampoon them and render them farcical and even evil. It is a truly strange thing to do and I as reader watched in disbelief as he seemed to lampoon his own novel.

Ophuls is introduced to us in romantic old Strasbourg, a worthy European counter to the magic of Kashmir. But totally missing is the rich, authentic detail with which Rushdie paints remote village life in Kashmir. He tries to replace it with stories about the heroic French resistance movement in Nazi-occupied France. But exaggerated anecdotes about wartime exploits do not fill the void left by lack of local detail. Rushdie quickly lapses into wide-eyed hyperbole of heroic exploits and inflates the abilities of his 'temporary' hero. Ophuls quickly begins to resemble an invincible American comic book hero or a British Biggles. He is rarely credible. Or much likable. Rushdie determines to build him up at all costs and begins dropping names, like Charles de Gaulle in his London exile. Ophuls becomes "the flying Jew" who can master the complex controls of a unique Bugatti fighter in a matter of seconds rather like James Boon 007 mastering his trick vehicles. He is a flawless academic, a superlative forger, an insuperable seducer and has, allegedly, bucketfuls of charm. This is how Rushdie wants us to see him here in these scenes. But in fact he is smug, unconvincing and a bore.

When he meets the love of his life—insofar as he is capable of loving anyone except himself—the plot goes absolutely loopy. Rushdie makes the bizarre decision that the beloved, a courageous, bold French resistance fighter by the name of Peggy Rhodes ("Ratty") who has allegedly killed a man with her bare hands (!), will talk like a demented Hugh Grant in one of his sillier romantic comedies. Her truncated staccato-speak is presumably meant to indicate an aristocratic English woman who seems very likely to say: "No sex, please, I'm British. Inhibited, you know. Bally silly, wot?" In fact she says far worse things than that.

Now the mainstream plot depends on this caricature of a British woman putting up bravely with her husband's 1,001 dalliances and one-night stands. He seems to suffer from prolonged Priapism. Even when he reaches the great old age of 80 he has learned absolutely nothing. He remains as insuperably vain and pompous as ever and still picks up a beautiful young Indian starlet, who is most improbably smitten with him, in his L.A. hotel's foyer. Together they have some highly improbable erotic dalliance, unless of course he has huge supplies of viagra hidden in the bathroom cabinet. This is very odd narrative indeed.

But long before all this nonsense in L.A., Max Ophuls' long-suffering British wife Peggy has finally left him and taken her revenge. Her revenge consists of stealing her husband's illegitimate child from his disgraced mistress the Hindu mother Boonyi. It is indeed sad that Ratty a heroine of the French WW II resistance should sink so low morally as to become a Rumpelstilzchen baby-snatcher. And that she does so while speaking the most ridiculous caricature of a British aristocrat's clipped, inhibited, no-nonsense speech patterns is unforgivable.

There is nothing that Peggy the resistance heroine of WW II has in common with the much older Peggy who steals Boonyi's baby. There is nothing that Ophuls the super-hero of the beginning of the novel has in common with Ophuls the anti-hero in the middle of the novel in Delhi. And there is nothing that Boonyi the lovable heroine of the Kashmiri beginning of the novel has in common with Boonyi the hideous anti-heroine in the Delhi middle of the novel. The characterization is hopelessly inconsistent and the only winner is the evident need of the plot for some sensational twists and turns.

It is as though, in this degrading section of the novel in Delhi, Rushdie is saying that he couldn't give a fig about the conventions in fiction that insist on consistency of character and consistency of genre. And certainly the laws of psychological realism with characters behaving in character and performing according to their established personality traits are thrown overboard. Max Ophuls, who was built up as a gallant and daring super-hero of the French resistance in WW II, now becomes nothing better than a name-dropping snob, an unscrupulous womanizer, a rutting goat and a cynical exploiter of a village girl. The contract into which he enters with Boonyi is played for cheap laughs by comparing it with the politicians' mania for contracts with acronyms. Even in old age he is an arrogant know-all and still fancies himself as a ladies' man at the age of eighty. His excessive vanity makes him easy prey for the assassin and frankly we are quite pleased to see him go.

With similar careless inconsistency, all the innocent charm and brave beauty of Boonyi, established in her village in Kashmir, is thrown away and suddenly she is made out to be depraved, lazy, greedy, immoral, shallow, and brainlessly self-indulgent as disillusion with her escape from provincial Kashmir to glamorous Delhi sets in. Her bargain with the devil brings her, predictably, very little. Her yearning for cosmopolitan adventure and glamour has brought her shame and futility because she is locked up in her dreadful rooms with no society and no friends.

For Rushdie, however, this fall is nowhere near enough. He now shows her falling victim in her depression to gluttony, then to pill-popping, and then to opium addiction. She doesn't just become fat—in an impossibly short period of time, one year or so?—she becomes so gargantuan that she is compared to a stranded whale who cannot fit through the doorway and who needs two seats in the aeroplane. But I always thought that opium addiction caused a wasting away and a complete loss of appetite. Are these dreadful scenes in Delhi just sloppy overwrite and grotesque farce on Rushdie's part? Of course in the genres of satire and parody, this kind of cruel farce and exaggerated caricature are all part of the fun. But as these ribald scenes come straight after a tender, lyrical portrait of Boonyi as a delicate, sensitive and brave lover in the moonlit fields of Kashmir, they are very offensive to the reader. Certainly I felt very cheated and was inclined to toss the novel out of the window. I was depressed that Rushdie, a very gifted storyteller, should leave me and the beautiful illusion that he had constructed so much in the lurch.

Perhaps Rushdie would counter that the age of psychological realism and consistency of character and genre is long since past. It has been superseded by magic realism, persistent intrusion of classical myth, facile hyperbole, strange twists of plot and comic book caricature. The fabulation is great but his inconsistency in the characterization of the major figures is poor.

It was therefore with considerable depression that I embarked on the second last section of the book entitled Shalimar the Clown. To my considerable amazement Boonyi's return to Kashmir heralds another violent reversal in the narrative technique. Abruptly and with very considerable talent Rushdie reverses the sloppy farce and grotesque scenes of Delhi. Instead he evokes a bone-chilling tragedy as Boonyi is informed that she has been declared to be dead by the villagers of Pachigam and she is forced to struggle through a snowstorm to live in ostracism like a witch in the deepest forest. This could easily have become melodrama, but because of the brilliant evocation of village superstitions, classical Hindu myths and the celebration of Kashmiri nature's magic power to heal, it comes across as moving tragedy. Boonyi is silently helped through the winter by the invisible assistance of the girl who had once been raped in Bonyi's place. She also in the intervening years has been virtually ostracized by the villagers because she is now polluted, even though through no fault of her own. Unlike Boonyi her banning from village intimacy and marriage is without blame on her part. Finally, Boonyi becomes an ascetic hermit longing in vain through repentance for a forgiveness that never comes.

Rushdie is not frightened to mix in some earthy humour with this high tragedy. One of the less attractive and less talented village girls set her cap at deserted and wifeless Shalimar the Clown and her clumsy manouverings are very funny. Back in Kashmir Rushdie the storyteller is back in his element.

It becomes clear that Rushdie has deliberately saved the most powerful writing for the last part of his saga. Many of the earlier sections, especially the shameful commercial-sexual liaison in Delhi now fade into insignificance. What the section 'Shalimar the Clown' offers towards the end of the story is the tragic destruction of the paradise Kashmir and the deadly effects of the polarization of Muslims and Hindus. What we are reading about is the virulent growth of religious and racial hatred, the flourishing of bigotry, fundamentalism, terrorist insurgencies and, in response, government-sanctioned militarist state-terrorism by the Indian army of occupation. Kashmir is no different from the tragic Balkanization of Yugoslavia and every bit as bloody, barbaric and ruthless. Rushdie's fictional evocation of this Balkanization is a masterpiece. Rushdie combines the grim denouement of the defiled marriage of Boonyi and Shalimar with the macro-story of the fall of beautiful, tolerant Kashmir into the hell of racial hatred and the primitive barbarism of attempted ethnic cleansing.

To summarize: Rushdie is a restless, postmodernist writer. He is intellectual, cultured, imaginative, but easily led into hyperbole and arabesques of decoration, farce and parody. He provides superb narrative entertainment and a kaleidoscope of moods, settings and mythically embroidered tales. For these reasons he is perhaps at his best with fabulations on the minor characters such as Maulana Bulbul Fakh, the witch Nazarebaddoor, Olga Volga, General Kachhwaha and Bombur Yambarzal. They are wonderful creations and some grotesque hyperbole does them no harm. But Rushdie does not seem to be close to his main characters and they do not always seem to be consistent or likeable. Entertaining, yes, emotionally complex but integrated personalities, no. We have already noted major character inconsistencies in the heroine Boonyi and in anti-hero Max Ophuls. We have already noted that Shalimar's characterization is very thin and it is amazing how much mileage Rushdie gets out of so little substance. But perhaps these are simply the limitations of postmodernist fabulation. Perhaps they don't even matter. Rushdie remains a master storyteller, a magic conjurer of moods and environments as varied as rural Kashmir, war-time Strasbourg, the slums of Los Angeles and death-row on San Quentin prison. Through all his extremes he takes his readers with him to a bizarre, heart-stopping finale. He is a superbly gifted fabulist.

Intertextuality: A Pattern of Similar Concerns in Raja Rao

RANU UNIYAL
Lucknow University, Lucknow

The novels of Raja Rao display the remarkable depth of the author's identification with the Indian ethos. His novels *Kanthapura, The Serpent and the Rope. The Cat and Shakespeare* and *Comrade Kirillov* are a testimony to his awareness of the Indian culture and milieu. His familiarity with the Indian traditions and his interest in the metaphysical reality, enable him to create such powerful and extraordinarily unique sagas of Indian reality. Raja Rao focuses on the individuals who have been estranged from the society in which they live and persistently explore the possibilities of overcoming such an estrangement. Raja Rao's "voluntary exile sharpened his awareness of his native heritage." (Naik in Rao, 144-45) His stay in France made him more conscious of the diversities which existed between the two cultures. The confrontation of the East with the West, both at political and cultural levels and the sharp distinction between the Gandhian and Marxian ideology are dealt with extensively in the novels of Raja Rao. The need to seek his roots in his native soil becomes so acute that one sees Raja Rao trying to revive the glorious Indian past through his characters.

Kanthapura was inspired by the struggle which ensued as a result of the movement led by Gandhi. In *Kanthapura*, the main cause of struggle is the systematic oppression of the Indians by the British. In *The Serpent and the Rope*, the protagonist desires to be himself, a need for self-exploration is too intense in him. In *Comrade Kirillov*, the individual 'P' uprooted from his native land seeks stability elsewhere. He turns into a communist and oscillates between excessive love for India on the one hand and commitment to Marxian ideology on the other. In all these major figures there is a desire to realize themselves by reviving the glorious Indian past. In *Kanthapura*, the struggle is triggered off by the reading of the Vedantic texts and the singing of bhajans. The protagonist Moorthy has created in the people a need for self-identity. The strong force of Indianness unites them and thus the fight against the colonial forces gains momentum. India to them signifies a powerful orbit in which their existence revolves. Faced with the same kind of conflicts and desires and a more or less similar anguish, the masses join hands with each other to oust the oppressive other, that is, the British. The signifying ensembles like 'Our country is being bled to death by foreigners. We have to protect our mother' (16), signify the need for self-preservation. Gandhiji's vision too said to Moorthy: "You can help your country by going and working among the dumb millions of the villages." (34) 'Dumb' as a connotative code signifies the state of mute existence of the oppressed beings under the authoritative other. Moorthy, growing aware of the forces of oppression repudiates their repressive tendencies. He gropes for a way out and under the influence of Gandhi he not only gives a clarion call for action but also that of self-reliance. 'Gandhi' is his guru and only after he surrenders himself before the guru is he able to realize the gravity of his mission. The protagonist refuses to be an object and the Red-man's tyranny over the Indian masses fills him with a growing hatred.

The protagonist Ramaswamy in *The Serpent and the Rope* is an individual who, though physically at a distance from India, is too close to it psychologically and not even the love of his wife Madeleine can retain him in France. A strong desire in him urges him to go back to his country. The given ensemble reveals his anguish at being away from the country: "For me India is Freedom." Rama was unable to be himself and wants to return to his soil to realize himself. So strong is this wish to go away from the alien world that he proposes to Madeleine to go to India, whereas she feels that to her "India is Paradise." The East is something unreal and unattainable and, therefore, she wishes to stay away from it. The East has an aura of mystery around it, therefore, the people from the West could not understand it completely. India remains incomprehensible and unapproachable to them. An enigma. A mystery. "India has no history, for Truth cannot have history." There is a gradual progression from Raja Rao's earlier treatment of struggle in *Kanthapura*, the struggle there was against colonial forces and to some extent Moorthy tried to analyze the basic cause of repression. The final truth which haunted him was:

> As long as there will be iron gates and barbed wires round the Skeffington Coffee Estate, and the city cars that can roll up the Bebbur mound, and gaslights and coolie cars, there will always be Pariahs and poverty. (181)

He protests and says: "it is the way of the masters that is wrong." (180-81) The protagonists in the novels of Raja Rao strive to collectively destroy the forces that threaten and undermine their existence. India to them represents the truth. Moorthy in *Kanthapura* emphasizes the value of truth. Truth is that strong weapon in the hands of an Indian which alone can bring change: 'Between truth and me none shall come.' (86)

> The whole of the Gangetic plain is one song of saintly sorrow, as though Truth began where sorrow was accepted, and India began where Truth was acknowledged.

Raja Rao believes in truth being God and according to Ramaswamy, who voices Rao's opinions, this truth resides in India. India to him symbolizes an abode of knowledge and nothing exists beyond this truth.

The quest for knowing himself is too deep-seated in Moorthy and Ramaswamy. In *Comrade Kirillov*, we come across an individual Padmanabhan Iyer who becomes a Communist after being appalled at the state of existence of men in Indian society. The presence of pariahs and the inhuman treatment meted out to them pricks his consciousness. Like Moorthy who was made to think: "How is one an outcaste?" (80) 'P' too thinks of the evils present in society and turns towards Marxism for a solution. The novel aims to show the protagonist in sheer confusion: 'a communist can be very sincere but his sincerity is confused. There is intellectual confusion,' states Raja Rao. (Niranjan, 58). P is lectual confusion,' states Raja Rao. (Niranjan, 58). P is caught between two opposing forces; on the one hand he believes that a revolution like the one in Soviet Union alone could solve the problems of Indians; on the other he feels proud of India's cultural heritage, for it has much to offer.

There is a desire in him to revive the Indian classics. Comparing the rich East with the shallow West, he says:

> Unlike Europe, it is not sincerity that goes a-begging in India—we are not yet that corrupt. But we shall soon reach the requisite standards. We are human like all. But one thing I felt sorry for when I was in India—the neglect of our classics. I forgot my politics for a time and jumped into the classics. It was such a joy to go back to *Uttarramacharita*, and to Kalidasa. (75)

Kirillov too, like Moorthy and Ramaswamy is very fond of India "his Indianhood would break through every community chain." (81) His being a communist did not in any way loosen his bonds with the Indian culture. There is a desire in him to see India free. Like Moorthy he pines for its freedom, but unlike him, he regards Marxism as the greatest possible weapon on earth. Future for him shall be bright only if one follows Communism and not Gandhism. He does not see eye to eye with Gandhian Ideology yet he extends blind support to him and is unable to hear a word uttered by the other against Gandhi:

> Kirillov was an Indian, and he had peculiar reactions which no dialectic could clarify. . . . He could not bear a word said against Mahatma Gandhi. (26)

This implies his subconscious love for Gandhi. Gandhi to him remained an epitome of goodness and love. There remains an affinity between Kirillov and Gandhi. He calls him:

> Friends and fool of the poor, the sadhu reactionary who still believed in caste and creed and such categories, and whose birth in this world had set history many centuries backwards. (53)

The protagonist Padmanabhan Iyer, later known as 'P' is torn between several conflicts. Raja Rao's three protagonists are Brahmins, Moorthy, Rama and 'P' who consciously try to bridge the ecart which existed between them and the others, yet are unable to give up their age-old beliefs. They are making vigorous attempts to realize their being and in this process undergo gradual transformation. To Ramaswamy 'Brahmin is he who knows Brahman.' (5)

A true Brahmin is one who seeks the ultimate truth and this can be attained only if he negates the other reality and probes into the inner one. There continues a constant search for the realizations of this truth. *Comrade Kirillov*, by becoming a communist, resorts to a new programme of action and hopes for a better India. He chooses to be a follower of Marx, just as Moorthy had chosen Gandhism as his form of action. His being a communist implies that he is on the side of the proletariat:

> Marxism had given a strange ascetic incision to his Brahminic manners and his sweetness had that unction, the theological compassion, of a catholic priest. (30)

But even the Marxian influence had not destroyed his faith in the concept of non-dualism. During moments of despair and crisis he would sing:

> Manobuddhi ahankara cittani naham
> cidananda rupah shivoham—shivoham. (86)

Uttering of 'I am Siva, I am Siva' provided him with strength. "Shivoham, Shivoham" as chanted by Moorthy, Ramaswamy and Kirillov, signifies the strong faith in the powers of the Supreme. Brahmin through the strong force of non-dualism, attains the highest state and in doing so realizes his entire being and thus knows perfect bliss, that is, himself. As we see Moorthy encouraging people to read Vedantic texts, Ramaswamy trying to explore the residues of meaning of life through them and Kirillov too showing interest in them we can feel Raja Rao himself trying to attain 'moksha' through non-dualistic approach. The entire thrust of the chanting of mantras is the supreme significance of a ritual action, through which the protagonist tries to assure himself of his existence on the earth. There is an underlying assumption that these individuals are torn between several conflicts and that the meticulous performance of several rituals like singing bhajans, reading religious books, going to the temple and discussing philosophy are essential to the proper understanding of one's self. The struggle becomes intense as the cultural affinity is established among people.

In his novels Raja Rao has also done a detached analysis of the relationship between the being and the other. The conflicts arise in the protagonists' mind due to several reasons. The struggle ensues not only between the British and the Indian, the East and the West, the Brahmins and the Pariahs, but it is also a struggle between man and woman to understand one another. Their inability to understand each other leads to several doubts and conflicts. The protagonist in Raja Rao's novels, through his relationship with the women, tries to analyze himself. All the female characters emerge as powerful individuals and their attitude towards life also brings a change in the behaviour of the protagonist. Woman is the other to him, and caught between the desire to possess the other and also to be free from the other, we find the protagonist going through several phases of uncertainty and confusion.

In *Kanthapura*, Moorthy's relationship with his mother is snapped off because of his progressive ideas. She, being an orthodox Brahmin, is unable to accept the fact that he had begun mixing with the pariahs. The dreams which she had built around him had no chance of being realized in the near future. He had given up his studies and his refusal to marry aggravates the tensions in her mind. Life to her becomes overshadowed with ennui and disappointment. The news of her son's ex-communication leaves her distressed. She accepts death as a consolation because she has nowhere to go. The unrelenting attitude of one leads to the complete destruction of the other.

As we analyze Moorthy's relationship with Ratna, Ramaswamy's relationship with Madeleine and Savithri, and Kirillov's relationship with Irene, we find the men in Raja Rao's novels unable to comprehend the mysterious other. Woman has always been revered and held in high esteem by these protagonists. She is a part of the reality on this earth. yet appears unreal and dream-like to the protagonist at times. Moorthy had loved Ratna but never disclosed his love for her. He realizes the power she has over him. Afraid of his being possessed by her, he refuses to be an object in his own eyes and the relationship takes a spiritual turn: 'she seemed something so feminine and soft and distant.' (64)

As she comes to see him, he realizes the impact of her presence on him. The struggle goes on in the mind of the protagonist. She appears to him as someone soft yet aloof. In his attempt to realize what feelings he had for her, we find Moorthy drifting away from the other. This distance, which gradually develops between the two on a physical level, does not separate them mentally. Moorthy, by refusing to succumb to his physical desires, is able to continue the freedom struggle and yet maintain an affinity with Ratna by writing to her. His writing a letter to her signifies the urgent need in him to be remembered and understood by the other.

The conflicts which arise in the mind of Ramaswamy due to his confrontation with the women are also responsible for creating the need for self-exploration in him. He marries Madeleine and even the strong bond of marriage does not let him penetrate the depths of her being. It was the Brahmin in him that had appealed to her. Ramaswamy tries to see himself in her: 'Madeleine was like the palace of Amber seen in moonlight . . . such a luminous mystery the deeper you go, the more you know yourself.' (14)

Ramaswamy has become so dependent on Madeleine that her absence makes life meaningless to him. On his return from India, Ramaswamy is unable to see Madeleine immediately and this leaves him estranged from the outer world:

> It makes all the difference in the world whether the woman of your life is with you or not; she alone enables you to be in a world that is familiar and whole. If it is not his wife, then for an Indian it may be a sister in Mysore, or little mother in Benares. (57)

It is her presence that makes the world a happy place to live in. The man in Raja Rao's novels discovers that he is helpless without her. Ramaswamy is attracted to the silence which makes her so different and yet so loving. Comparing Madeleine to his little mother he says, "they both had the same shy presence, both rather silent and remembering everything; they loved, too, more than is customary." (20) Of Savithri he says, "she never says anything that really matters and, her presence never said anything, but her absence spoke." (31)

The mutual passion between Ramaswamy and Savithri creates their own world, separate from others: "for her, I could see, everything was gesture and symbol . . . all was secret to her but herself—so all was a legend, and every event a wonder." (126)

During her visit to France, Savithri's relationship with Ramaswamy takes on a spiritual aspect. He gives her the toe rings of his mother. The spiritual marriage between the two signifies their desire to remain rooted to their innermost self. Even his sister Saroja appears as an unknown being to Ramaswamy. There was this desire in her: 'to hide something of her own.' (49) The silence of the woman as a significant sign can be conceived as a bearer of meaning. Through her 'silence' one can give meaning to several other actions of hers. A woman is that incomprehensible other and in Madeleine we find a desire to own Ramaswamy. She treats him like a god and worships him: "To amount oneself in worshipping another is the basis of all love. We become ourself by becoming another." (81) Just as Ratna worshipped Moorthy and was willing to do anything for him, we can see an attitude of subservience visible in Madeleine. Deep down in her heart lies the wish to possess him. This realization that she understands him far too well grips Rama with fear: "I could be bent by the knowledge she had of me—the knowledge of my silences, the vigorous twists of my mental domain." (92) As Sartre has also pointed: "There is a relation of the for-itself with the in-itself in the presence of the other." (92) She loved him and was conscious of the desire to grab hold of his being. Love becomes an enterprise to her. It is an attempt at realizing herself and this leads to her alienation with the other.

She talked of him to the others like Tante Zoubie and Catharine and says:

> I spoke especially of the respect you show to me—for you, a woman is still the other, the strange, the miracle. You could never show the familiarity European men show, towards their wives. You worship women even if you torture them. But I like to be tortured and to be your slave. (98)

This confession of Madeleine reveals her inner sight. Analyzing this sort of relationship, Sartre says: "in love the lover wants to be 'the whole world' for the beloved. This means that he puts himself on the side of the world." (479) The protagonist on having realized the incompatibility between him and the other refuses to become an object for what he wants is different from what the other can give: "No, of course I did not want a slave. I wanted a companion of pilgrimage." (98)

Gradually we see the protagonist Rama trying to understand the philosophy of life. He severs all connections with Madeleine and decides to come back to India. He feels: "Life is made for woman—man is a stranger on this earth." This realization, that a woman is intimate to another woman in a way a man could never be to another man, fills Ramaswamy with a sense of isolation. His entire being finds itself alienated from the material world and the search for the unknown persists. He finally comes to a conclusion that what separated him from Madeleine was India. India he feels stands "vertical to space and time, and is present at all points."

'India' to Ramaswamy represents that whole beyond which lies no other truth. 'India' as a socio-cultural code represents not only Brahmin but also the absolute. The protagonist after having been unable to identify himself with the West pines to go back to his roots. It is the Indianness in him which makes him accept the superiority of woman over the other. She represents an entirety to him.

The woman, therefore, to Ramaswamy represents not only the 'Panch Tatvas' but also the entire universe. It is only through his contacts with the other that Ramaswamy realizes the final truth. Life and death to him appear as the two integrated forces and there remains continuity between the two. The revelation to the protagonist comes as a surprise. He discovers his inner contradictions. As a being he knows he possesses the capacity to transcend his present situation and its possible limitations. Yet part of his individuality is infected with a desire to be loved and this seems paradoxical. He accepts what he wants and says in his diary: "5.5.54. 'No' not a God but a Guru is what I need." (34) To such a Guru he was taken. The Guru, he tells Madeleine can let him distinguish the Serpent from the Rope. He alone would be able to light his path and lead him towards perfect bliss i.e. attainment of the absolute. For him: 'India is the Guru of the world.' (332)

Thus we see that the protagonist in *The Serpent and the Rope* is in quest of the ultimate reality. He discovers at last that the problems he is facing have a spiritual connotation and this unrest due to spiritual conflict in the mind cannot be easily resolved. His pilgrimage ends with the discovery of truth, the Guru. Self-knowledge being the goal of his life, he decided to return to India for complete discovery of oneself.

This crucial need to understand, results from a slow evolution in Raja Rao's thought. In *Kanthapura*, Moorthy, after having understood that change alone would result in proper freedom, raises his voice against the inequality which exists in society at several levels. In *The Serpent and the Rope*, Ramaswamy's predicament and his ultimate realization of what he wants from life resulted from his ties with his past, the irresistible urge in him to go back to India from France and his incapacity to give up his Indian identity. The implication being that his quest for knowledge could never be fulfilled unless he found a Guru an epitome of truth and this truth resides only in India.

Comrade Kirillov is much more than the chronicle of an Indian turned Marxist. The book reveals the conflict of commitments. In *Comrade Kirillov*, we find Padmanabhan Iyer trying to adhere to the communist programmes. By doing so he tries to break away from the old order and bring in a revolution. In communism lies an answer to all human problems. He derives his conviction from Marx but this alone does not fulfil his being in totality. We see 'P' caught between several unsolvable dilemmas. Even communism is unable to give an answer to his questions. His love for India draws him back to its roots. Proud of its cultural heritage, he finds it difficult to break away from the familiar grounds. The protagonist in *Comrade Kirillov* is unable to set himself free from all bonds of Indianhood. 'He was ever conscious of his skin' in England. After having been treated as a mere object of ridicule by the British,

> The brahminic sensibility of Kirillov had such antennae inward and outward that a fierce anger rose in his belly. And he cursed the British race, wished it a sepulchral fire, and the red, ruinous tongue of Hell. (52)

Comrade Kirillov's hatred towards the British is too intense and he wishes their complete extirpation. Both Moorthy and Kirillov strive for a change in society. Nevertheless they differ in their ideologies. Moorthy, a follower of Gandhi, believes in non-violence and hopes to transform the enemy through love. *Comrade Kirillov* however feels contempt for British race and believes:

> The communist, the true Marxist, is above all a realist. . . . Mahatma Gandhi should have been born in the Middle Ages, and he should not have bothered us with his theology in this rational age of ours. (37)

Like Moorthy, he craves for a classless society where all individuals would be their own masters and wealth be equally distributed among them. To him communism is a genuine resolution of the conflict between one man and the other.

A brief survey of *The Cat and Shakespeare* reveals that it is a sequel to Raja Rao's other novels. Raja Rao calls it 'a metaphysical comedy.' The author has tried to give a comic flavour to serious philosophical issues. The protagonist Ramakrishna Pai is advised by Govindan Nair not to worry for:

> Life is a riddle that can be solved with a riddle. You can remove a thorn with another thorn, you solve one problem through another problem. Thus the world is connected. (37)

The woman to the protagonist always remains 'a puzzle.' The novel is full of symbolic allusions from the Upanishad and parables taken from the Puranas. The life to Govindan Nair is 'a rationshop' and "Shakespeare knew every mystery of the rationshop." (83) Shakespeare's penetrating soul had looked deep into the recesses of human thought. The 'cat' in the novel is a symbol with multiple implications as the *Prakriti* or the Mother or the Guru or the Divine. The brief narrative while trying to grapple with a wide range of ideas has become too complex and obscure to an ordinary reader.

The protagonist is seen in search of an answer to his existential predicament. Various questions haunt him. However, all of them have only one answer and that lies in the discovery of the divine. His final realization is that God alone can save the world from peril and complete resignation to him can provide salvation to the searching souls. He realizes that "the unknown alone resolves the unknown." *The Cat and Shakespeare*, as Naik puts it, "has its moments of dazzling brilliance and sudden glory, but the brief blinding lighting flash, with its searing white splendour, though impressive, can never take the place of the midday sun." (142)

The most striking feature in the novels of Raja Rao is his use of a variety of signs and symbols which embody a vast network of meaning. Through the use of signs and symbols not only has he probed the personal and cultural relationships which form the basis of our social codes but also hidden, secret recesses of the human psyche.

The characters in his novel come alive through the narrative process. In *Kanthapura*, an old woman is narrating the villager's struggle for freedom. The narrator's style may seem tediously repetitive to the hasty reader, but this is not so: the manner in which she unfolds the story forms the very essence of the novel. The narrator, Achakka, subtly draws our attention to an interminable tale where one episode follows another and gradually the problematics is unfolded. Raja Rao tries to justify his technique when he says: "Our method of expression therefore has to be a dialect which will some day prove to be as distinctive and colourful as the Irish or the American. Time alone will justify it." (Author's Foreword to *Kanthapura*)

The people in *Kanthapura* after having launched a struggle against existing inequalities try to strengthen their political consciousness by seeking socio-cultural integration. Raja Rao has focussed on several important problems of the society. Raja Rao successfully highlights certain socio-economic issues which have been responsible for cultural and political estrangement.

The characters in *Kanthapura* strive to eliminate certain social evils like untouchability, social inferiority of women, suppression of widows, those rites and practices which hinder the national character of the struggle. The protagonist Moorthy is seen pondering: "How is one an outcaste?" The women of *Kanthapura* refuse to be submissive and fight vigorously for their upliftment. Once an awareness of their state of suppression is created in them they begin questioning themselves: "How can we be, like we used to be ?" Moorthy realizes the futility of freedom as long as there is economic disparity among men. His final question: "What is the goal?" leaves one disgusted with the ruling class.

The Gandhian struggle brings about many profound changes in the life of the people. Once they discover their rich cultural values they acquire a clearer awareness of the economic realities of the country and the sufferings of the common people. Thus we see people in Raja Rao's *Kanthapura* striving for political independence which would also include their economic, social and cultural progress.

The final realization dawns upon Moorthy that no political liberty can come without the inner being achieving freedom. The novels of Raja Rao portray such protagonists who try to resolve their inner turmoil. Their psychological upheavals are caused by forces both within and without. They begin their journey, the exodus towards the realm of self-knowledge. Ignorance of the self as well as the tentacles of society are the sources of man's misery. The means to resolve such issues appear too idealistic; we notice that the author's protagonists embody the futile meanderings in a labyrinth of darkness that occasionally admits a streak of hope.

Works Cited

Naik, M.K. *Raja Rao*. New York: Twayne, 1972.

_____. *A History of Indian English Literature.* Delhi: Sahitya Akademi, 1982.

_____. *Perspectives on Indian Fiction in English.* Delhi: Abhinav, 1985.

Niranjan, Shiva. *Novelist as Sadhaka.* Ghaziabad: Vimal, 1985.

Raja Rao. *Kanthapura.* London: George Allen and Unwin, 1938; New York: New Directions, 1963.

_____. *The Serpent and the Rope.* London: John Murray, 1960; Delhi: Hind Pocket Books, Orient Paperbacks, 1968.

_____. *The Cat and Shakespeare: A Tale of Modern India.* New Delhi: Vision Books, Orient Paperbacks, 1971.

_____. *Comrade Kirillov.* New Delhi: Vision Books, Orient Paperbacks, 1978.

Sartre, J.P. *Being and Nothingness.* New York: Washington Square Press Pocket Books, 1968.

Looking at History through the Magnifying Glass: Mukul Kesavan's *Looking through Glass*

TAPAN K. GHOSH
University of Burdwan

In his seminal essay, 'Outside the Whale,'[1] Salman Rushdie makes a fuss about the recent spate in England of fictions and movies about the British Raj and the zombie-like revival of the defunct empire. 'The recrudescence of imperialist ideology' at a time when Britain is faced with the danger of cultural psychosis, is, according to the midnight's child, a part of a 'revisionist enterprise.' The main objectives of this project are to refurbish the tarnished image of the empire, to exculpate the race of its historic guilt, and to propagate that 'the British weren't as bad as people make out,' that 'British Empire represented something noble or great about Britain,' and that it was, 'in spite of all its flaws and meanness and bigotries, fundamentally glamorous.' The propagation of this revisionist theory and the presentation of a false, exotic orient in these fictions and movies (like 'Gandhi,' 'The Far Pavilions, and 'Jewel in the Crown') have been directed at providing 'moral, cultural and artistic justification for imperialism and for its underpinning ideology, that of the racial superiority of the Caucasian over the Asiatic.' Rejecting the political quietism recommended by George Orwell in *Inside the Whale*, Rushdie who claims to be 'radioactive with history and politics,' proposes to quarrel, 'as loudly and as embarrassingly as possible,' with such false notions of (Indian) history.

Yes, quarrel we must, with English fictions written in India and abroad about India and her colonial past that seek to present a revisionist, even prejudiced, history of the country, if we are not ashamed of our nation and national struggle for Independence. The occasion for such a remark is provided by a detailed reading of Mukul Kesavan's overrated novel, *Looking through the Glass*, which created quite a stir in 1995. The publication of this high-profile novel was a literary event. It was the British Publishing Industry's 'Novel from India for 1994-95,' and there was much media hype that it would be short-listed for the Booker Prize. The book had 'soared into the empyrean even before being published'[2] and was acclaimed as 'the finest first novel ever written by an Indian in English,'[3] 'a stunning novel'[4] and 'a first novel by a brilliant, superlatively talented writer.'[5] All these critical clichés together with the much-publicized meeting of Kesavan with Salman Rushdie in London during the former's book-promotion tour, prepare the readers of Indian English fiction for something unprecedented. But this expectation is not fulfilled by the novel itself, by what happens within its pages, thus confirming one's suspicion that the attention *Looking through Glass*, much like Vikram Seth's *A Suitable Boy*, received had little to do with its literary merits.

What happens in the book that took Kesavan ten years to complete and that was based on his extensive research on the communal politics of U.P. in the last decade of Indian struggle for Independence? Set in the troubled and communally charged 1940s, the novel examines the dilemma of North Indian Muslims who equally distrusted the Congress and the Muslim League and to whom the idea of Partition and of a separate Muslim state was unpalatable because they were culturally and economically rooted in the place they lived in (it is Lucknow in Kesavan's fictional world). The issue of roots, which has no reference to the community, and the tragedy of Partition that made millions of people deracinated and join what Larry Collins and Dominique Lapierre call 'the greatest migration in history,'[6] have been superbly dealt with in Rahi Masoom Raza's *Adha Gaon*, Badiuzzama's *Chaako ki Wapsi*, Kamaleshwar's *Registan*, Bhisham Sahni's *Tamas*. But whereas the indigenous sensibilities of these regional writers dramatize the psychological trauma of Partition and the overwhelming agony of forceful removal of people from their 'watan,' the Western trained imagination of Kesavan totally leaves out the inner lives of the characters. Like Milan Kundera, he seems to have little use for psychological novel in which the motives of the characters are central. Depriving characters, set in a political tragedy, of an interior landscape and interweaving private lives and public events into one comic framework are something one frequently comes across in the novels of the Czech writer. *Looking through Glass* is a unique novel that deals with the historical perspective of the country's vivisection on the communal basis without attempting to capture the psychological landscape of the times. It is a 'comic epic'[7] that focuses through magic realist techniques how the immense possibilities in the country's past were squandered by petti-fogging and communally-biased politicians of the Congress and the Muslim League. There is no reference in the book to the imperialistic designs of the British, their satanic mischief and abominable complicity in the communal politics that throttled the nationalist aspirations for a secular, united and democratic India. In Kesavan's version of history, the Congress under the stewardship of Mahatma Gandhi had side-stepped the secular Muslims in favour of the (Hindu) masses: the idiom of Congress politics was borrowed from the Hindu religious ethos; the Quit India Movement was only an abortive expression of Hindu nationalism and cultural rhetoric to which Indian Muslims remained by and large indifferent. Here Nehru is projected as an 'usutper,'[8] (369) Maulana Abul Kalam Azad as a 'showboy' (314) of the Congress, and Jinnah, the author of the Two-Nation Theory, as 'avuncular, grave, aloof and kind.' (117) The honors of Partition are stripped of their tragic edge in the fictional narration and the novel seems completely inoculated against violence and atrocity. The reason of this pious attempt to mitigate the violent awfulness of Partition is the author's belief that "there is some sense in which we'll never take in the real horror of Partition. Unlike the Holocaust, it is not sufficiently stigmatized as evil. . . . Because there's no one to clearly blame . . . [and] the whole demonology is different."[9] All this is very good. One only feels a little sad for those countless writers on both sides of the international border, the likes of Yash Pal, Saadat Hasan Manto, Kartar Singh Duggal, Bhisham Sahni, and Samaresh Basu—who have fictionalized 'the single most traumatic experience'[10] in the recent history of the subcontinent, and the unprecedented violence it unleashed in an impartial, balanced manner, although few of them have succeeded in avoiding sentimentalism and maintaining—like Manto, for example—a cool, ironic distance.

In the very opening chapter of *Looking through Glass* the style is firmly set. It is that of magic realism, of which Rushdie is now regarded as the best exponent from the Third World. It is being held out by many postcolonial writers as the only proper form for the Third World novel, and recent history is assumed in them to be its only legitimate subject. The recipe is very familiar: linking personal history with public events and presenting the experience of an individual or a family or a group as the experience of a country; stressing the historical centrality of the narrator (Rushdie's oft-quoted formulation in the opening page of *Midnight's Children* is: "I had been mysteriously handcuffed to history, my destinies indissoluble chained to those of my country."[11]); the interpenetration of multiple realities—the fantastic or the improbable, the fictitious, the banal and the realistic in the stream of the narrator's consciousness; the simultaneity of the past and the present; and the substitution of private version of history for objective reality (that includes, among other things, distortion and revision of official and generally accepted history—a process immortalized in *Midnight's Children* by Rushdie's formulation, 'chutneyfication' of history: "I'm prepared to distort everything to re-write the whole history of my times purely in order to place myself in a central role."[12]) The forms of narrativization in these novels are basically non-mimetic and occasionally marked, as in Rushdie, by digressive self-reflexivity. Aijaz Ahmed writes in his book, *In Theory: Classes, Nations, Literatures:* "The essential task of a 'Third World' novel, it is said, is to give appropriate form (preferably allegory, but epic also, or fairytale, or whatever) to the national experience."[13] This kind of novel raises particular kind of questions relating to colonialism, the 'myth' of nation and national leaders, and postcoloniality. Timothy Brennan has categorized these writers as 'Third World Cosmopolitans,' 'those writers western reviewers seemed to be choosing as the interpreters and authentic public voices of the Third World.'[14]

For a long time in western literary criticism the term 'mirror' and 'glass' were used in a special sense in any discussion of mimetic narration. From Plato to the eighteenth century the generally accepted concept of literature was that it was a 'mirror' or imitation of life. The term 'mimesis'—Plato's word for imitation—was also used by Aristotle in his *Poetics*, although in a slightly different sense. Like other literary genres, the novel also reflected 'a no-nonsense kind of mimetic realism, a quasi-scientific explanation of the way the world worked and a firm sense of moral and social responsibility.'[15] But things changed with the publication of two books in the late 19th century by Oxford Professor, Charles Lutwidge Dodgson (1832-98), under the pen-name Lewis Carroll: *Alice in Wonderland* (1865) and *Through the Looking Glass* (1871). The term 'glass' is used in an altogether different sense in Caroll's works. The glass reflects persons and things standing before it more or less faithfully. But if one enters inside the glass and looks through it? Curious things will happen. One will find oneself, like Alice, in a wonderland which is absurd, grotesque and fantastic. Kesavan's novel looks at an important part of Indian history through the looking glass and lands his readers in a world that has elements of fantasy in it and that constantly challenges our notion of the real world. It is a world where the narrator meets his own grandmother whom he had cremated only a short while ago, where Muslims periodically disappear and Hindus go through the process of mutation, thus assuming multiple, ambiguous identities.

In the novel, the camera serves a metaphorical function. The narrator tells the story of his life in terms of photography and sees everything—the decaying British Raj, the Quit India Movement, and the historical perspective of Partition—through the zoom lens of his camera:

> But there was a price I paid for those pictures; an hour of every visit was spent listening patiently to Dadi's first person account of the struggle for Independence. In the early days it was an epic tale; she gave me a wide-angle picture of the Gandhian decades, but af-

ter the first few visits she zoomed in on the great Salt Satyagraha led by the Mahatma in 1930. (2)

The narrator, an ambitious Hindu photographer, is at the beginning unconcerned with history. But with the progress of the narrative history claims him for its own and he finds himself translated, borne across time, in the troubled forties. It is difficult to separate the narrator from the author in this book. Consequently, it seems to be an autobiographical novel.[16] Kesavan's fictional narrative may be fabricated but the world his characters inhabit is certainly not. The names of the places, through which the narrator makes his odyssey in an alien time and the principal characters of the drama of Partition, are historical. The author has consciously left no scope for fictionalization, as Rushdie has done in *Shame*.

The period of external history that the narrative covers is the last six years of the Indian struggle for freedom. It begins with the historic Quit India rebellion and ends with Partition. There are also references to the Khilafat movement, the Mappila rebellion in Malabar in 1920s, and the Salt Satyagraha in early 1930s.

The novel begins with the narrator's train journey to Benaras to tip the ashes of his illustrious grandmother into the Ganga. A self-reliant woman of exceptional integrity, Dadi had answered Gandhiji's call for civil disobedience by picketing liquor shops and spent six months in the colonial jail with her unweaned son at her breast. But this grand woman, who 'had grown used to paying her tithe to the Nation in the coin of social work,' (4) was later consumed by guilt for her failure to participate in the Quit India Movement due to familial constraints: "The August rebellion became a black hole in her memory that sucked in everything that ever happened to her afterwards, that collapsed her entire life into a single non-event." (6)

At some point in his journey, the narrator steps down from the train to look through his camera's magic eye at 'the world close-up from an invulnerable distance.' (8) He tumbles through the glass into the river and lands in another world at another time. It is Lucknow of August 1942, and the Quit India rebellion is sweeping through the Gangetic plains. Stuck in a world not of his own choosing, he feigns amnesia and decides to remain perfectly insulated from everything around him till he returns to his mislaid present, to his own time with its black and white simplicity. But in the course of his 'promiscuous drifting through this alien time, infecting more and more of it with [his] presence and being lathered by its dust in return,' (39-40) he discovers that his displacement in time is irreversible. A 'homeless waif' (14) without a name, he improvises a life and assembles a world around him. In the course of his involuntary peregrination during the last years of the crumbling Raj, he acquires a strange foster family, makes some uncommon friends and witnesses some momentous events that defined the last phase of the Indian struggle for Independence. His life becomes inextricably linked with the fates of these idiosyncratic people who populate Kesavan's fictional world. The members of his foster family, like some of his acquaintances in this fabulous world, are endowed with multiple, ambiguous religious identities at a time when the entire subcontinent is divided along communal lines. They are Muslims but Hindus, Hindus mutated into Islam. They are secular, hospitable, affectionate, and totally untouched by communal prejudice or bigotry. Ammi, sceptical about change and filled with Old World certitudes; Masroor, desperate to stall Hindu-Muslim riots, 'deaf to large ideas and blind to crusading visions,' (255) a seeker of a free, united and secular India, who feels himself let down by the Congress which has alienated the nationalist Muslims by its failure to address their insecurities, and finally goes over to the Muslim League; Asharfi, whose undefined, unfocussed yearnings find consummation in lesbian love and erotic painting. They are forever waiting for their patriarch, Intezar, who had vanished during his pilgrimage to Mecca, to return. A Kashmiri Brahmin domiciled in Lucknow, Intezar (Charandas Ganjoo was his real name) convened to Islamic spiritualism by his passion for Urdu poetry and his love for Kulsum, the daughter of an eminent Urdu poet. The family's well-wisher is Haasan, presumed to be a Muslim by many but who is actually a middle-aged Iyengar Hindu (Haasan being his ancestral place name), who reached Lucknow in 1921 as a coffee house manager after a series of fantastic adventures that had developed in him a strong distaste for the brahminical notion of purity and consistency. He was branded like a cow with the logo of Hindu faith—Swastika—by a group of Hindu fanatics who had mistaken him for a Muslim. The horrible experience had effected a transformation in Haasan and generated in him 'a love for essential humanity, unclassified, unclothed.' (85) Among the narrator's acquaintances are Chaubey, a revolutionary leader turned sexual gymnast ending his life as a human cannonball; Gyanendra, a lecherous scoundrel masquerading as religious professional who harbours a senile fantasy of filming 'Kamasutra'; and Parwana, a girl of obscure origins whose life took off from a Bombay orphanage to be ravaged in the name of realism (she nearly lost her life in a make-believe pyre as an ersatz sati in a film studio) and ravished in the name of fantasy (raped by Gyanendra's repertory star Chaubey) and who ultimately finds refuge in a home for fallen women run by the narrator's grandmother. The story woven around these characters is a fantastic one—a mixture of comedy and farce, friendship and repulsion, hope and despair. The novelist has 'treated these characters like flesh and blood equals, as free, self-willed individuals carving out their destinies.' (52) But, in actuality, they are no better than 'cardboard figures playing bit roles in a tightly scripted play [with] a happy ending.' (52) He takes them through Lucknow, Banaras, Delhi and Simla—the exact area of Kesavan's research on pre-Partition communal politics—until the narrative culminates in the climactic moment of Partition. In the course of his picaresque wanderings, the narrator participates in the Quit India rebellion as 'Dadi's proxy,' (101) witnesses the violence perpetrated by 'Gandhi's rabble' (66) ('the faceless, faithless, rampant masses' [252]) and the Muslim indifference to the Congress politics, and waits on Jinnah and the Muslim League Delegation to the Simla Conference as a waiter in a British hotel. Meanwhile, the 'gigantic surge of history' (16) propels him and his improvised world inexorably to the foredoomed finale in August 1947. This is the key to the fictional tension in *Looking through Glass*, 'the tragic scope of Kesavan's protagonist living through a period of history that has already been written.'[17] It is the tragedy of hindsight:

> I was warmed by pity, not only because they had lost Masroor but because the end of the world they knew was due. In less than five years there would be murder, arson, rape, flight, migration, butchered trains, refugees, dispossession, enemy aliens . . . in short, Partition. And here they were Asharfi, Ammi and Haasan, living in the lull and thinking it the storm. It made me feel omniscient; I felt like a historian brought up face to face with some lost cause, some extinct line that he had chronicled. (51-52)

Having lost his world once, he desperately tries to protect his foster family, which has given him an identity and a refuge in this alien time from the impending catastrophe. Like a 'maverick hero,' (332) he tries to 'play matador to a fury' (284) that will split a million families in the wake of Partition, and makes some Quixotic plans to disable the known course of events, not for the whole nation, because he is not concerned about the fates of others, but for his Muslim friends:

> I wasn't worried for myself. I had been born a Hindu and in Delhi from all accounts it was mainly Muslims who died. Nor was I concerned about India because it was difficult to feel for a subcontinent. I was just worried for my friends in Lucknow. Not for Haasan since he was a Hindu too, but for Ammi and Asharfi, and Masroor. (174-75)

He is not worried for his grandmother because 'she was a Hindu'; Parwana is none of his business. In the wake of a 'pogrom of Muslims in Delhi' (352) during the Partition, the authorities round up the Muslims for their safety and keep them in the Old Fort, away from the wrath of Hindu zealots:

> Within the Fort . . . a single species, Homo islamicus, had been corralled for its own safety and well-being. A superior zoo, progressive and opposed to cages, because its charges were being held only till they could be released into their natural habitat, which was then being fenced a few hundred miles away. (216)

The refugees are given the choice to decide their nationality and most of them decide in favour of Pakistan. The Ganjoo family remains undecided because of division of opinion among its members. While Ammi, who is averse to the large ideas of change and wants to preserve the world as it is, rejects Pakistan because it won't be Lucknow, (330) Masroor, disillusioned by the Congress betrayal, prefers the Muslim Homeland. The novel ends on an up-beat note with the return of Intezar, like the Mahdi figure (Redeemer) in Islam, from hiding at the crucial moment and his presence solves the problem of choice for his family, because 'Intezar was home.' (373)

Beneath all the magic-realist pyro-techniques, spoof and sexual gymnastics that the novel encompasses, there is an attempt at a metaphorical examination of Indian identity which is based on the notion of multiplicity, hybridity and religious tolerance and immune from bigotry, communal prejudice and invocations of purity and consistency which were at the root of the communal division of the country which ultimately led to the Partition. This ideological function is served in the novel by Haasan, Intezar and, to some extent, the narrator himself. At one point in the narrative, the protagonist, reflecting on the Muslim League's call for a separate Muslim state, says:

> Like other secular people in independent India I had been brought up to believe that religion was a private matter confined to the inner space between brains and bowels, so it couldn't possibly make a difference to arse-washing techniques which fell outside its scope in the secular realm. I was also taught that differences were unimportant since we were all identical in our essential humanity. (175)

This commendable intent notwithstanding, the book reveals a clear bias in its presentation of the history of Indian struggle for freedom. By fabricating a set of characters 'whose social contract has everything to do with contingency,'[18] Kesavan makes an unambiguous statement, an unmistakable political choice. His bias is reflected in the preferential treatment of the people of a particular faith (contrast Hassan's farcical treatment of the brahminical fetish for purity [79-80], with that of Bihari Halvai's reverential attitude to Jamal Mian's Islamic faith [45]); the juxtaposition of Ramlila and Kamasutra; the lop-sided portrayal of the Muslim problem before the Partition; the presentation of the Quit India rebellion, which shook the nation as nothing else did and in which, for all we know, Muslims also participated,[19] as an expression of Hindu cultural nationalism (of which the Congress was the exponent); the denigration of Mahatma's clarion call: 'Do or die,' and the caricature of Congress workers, who appear no better than figures in a meagrely animated cartoon. (234) Certain parts of the book, which attempt to create fictional equivalents of the literal facts of history, tend too much to parody (note, for example, the siege of Madhuban in the chapter entitled '2000 A.V.'). One is astonished by the historical accuracy of the setting in some places (see, for instance, the Simla Conference [312-16] which seems to have been lifted from textbook history). But even more surprising are a number of factual errors that one comes across in Kesavan's narrative. About the pre-Partition riots in Bengal, the narrator, who is deeply worried about the fates of his Muslim friends, says:

> At the end of July Jinnah called upon Muslims to celebrate 16 August as Direct Action Day. Nobody knew what that meant till the day rolled round and the killings began in Calcutta. Even that didn't disturb me much because Calcutta was a thousand miles away. Then some more were killed in Noakhali, but for me that was Bangladesh and someone else's country. (351-52)

Noakhali in August 1946 was in Bangladesh! And Gandhiji, Mountbatten's 'One Man Boundary Force,'[20] risked his own life to dissolve communal tension and preach Hindu-Muslim amity in someone else's country'! Most of the peasants dying in Bengal during the famine of 1942 were, a British Clerk informs the readers, Muslims (294). After his return from 'limbo' into which Masroor, like thousands of 'Congress Muslims' had gone during the Quit India rebellion due to the apathy of the party to their anxiety and insecurity, he joins the Muslim League paper, *Dawn*, as a sports reporter and he starts 'with a series of profiles: Great Pakistani Cricketers: Past and Present.' (254) Pakistani cricketers in 1942! Rushdie, it is well known, also commits factual inaccuracy in dating the assassination of Mahatma Gandhi in *Mid-*

night's Children. But then, that is Saleem Sinai's version of history and he deliberately flouts the conventions of historical writing to place himself in a central position.

Indeed, the shadow of Rushdie looms very large in *Looking through Glass*. In his interview with *Indian Review of Books*,[21] Kesavan admits the stylistic influence of Rushdie on his novel. There are a number of unambiguous echoes of *Midnight s Children* in it: the interpenetration of the individual or familial history with the history of the nation, the unstable and shifting identities of characters, the disappearance of the Muslims during the Quit India movement, the narrator's amnesia and his voluntary circumcision towards the end, Masroor's doubt-planting machine and jigsaw designed 'to teach Congressmen that they were dropping their Muslim pieces,' (230) and the dinner table conclave of the Muslim League in Simla (remember the pepper-pot episode?). Not to mention the Rushdie-like penchant for vulgarity and crudity, frottage and voyeurism, and infantile attempt at parody:

> Long years ago, according to Nehru, he and some others had made a tryst with Destiny, but Masroor didn't have an appointment with anyone quite as grand. All he had were the date palms. Some weeks ago I made a date with date palms . . . he could have said. (362)

Apart from these magic realist techniques, Kesavan's novel reminds one of Rushdie in another significant way. *Looking through Glass* is a stringent critique of Congress policies in 1942. Various characters voice their—and also their creator's—disapproval of the national leaders' fetish about change and progress and their grand visions which proved disastrous for the uncommitted masses. This distrust of grand public events which jeopardize individual lives is also voiced by Rushdie's protagonist:

> Politics, children: at the best of times a bad dirty business. We should have avoided it, I should never have dreamed of purpose. I am coming to the conclusion that privacy, the small individual

> lives of men, is preferable to all this inflated macrocosmic activity.[22]

One only wonders whether the struggle against colonialism, and the independence of the country—however moth-nibbled it might be—would have been possible if some persons had not possessed grand visions and inspired a prostrate people with self-respect, self-reliance, and dreams of a bright future. There is no serious attempt, in *Looking through Glass*, at an objective examination of the reasons why the nation's dream had gone sour, as there is no reference to the British collusion with Jinnah's two-nation theory which accelerated the communal division of the subcontinent and in which, if we are to believe Maulana Azad's testimony in *India Wins Freedom*, Nehru and Sardar Patel had acquiesced. It is a Partition novel written on an epic scale that remains silent about what happened during those fateful days and months after the country's 'tryst with Destiny' on the other side of Radcliffe's boundary, one in which Gandhi is presented as a leader of the Hindu masses who was blind to the Muslim problem in the country ('Suddenly the Muslim mind became close to him, suddenly the masses became irresistibly urgent.' [247]), the same Gandhi who was assassinated by Hindu fanatics for his supposed love for Muslims. Even Rushdie would have hesitated to project the father of the nation as communally biased. For, despite his slips and peccadilloes, his hymns to chutney and chutneyfication, Salim Sinai is able to establish himself as an unprejudiced observer of the politics of India and Pakistan. His views of politics and of the relentless march of history that tramples individual lives, are neither Hindu nor Muslim, neither Indian nor Pakistani. He reacts to historical events from a purely human point of view that transcends nationality, political creed and cultural upbringing. It is this quintessential humanism that makes him feel responsible for whatever happens in the political arena. But Kesavan, by making his political choice very clear, abdicates his role as an impartial chronicler and commentator of Indian history.

One wonders what this much-flaunted book realizes after all. What emerges from it in terms of history and literature? What does it mediate in terms of experience? The Indian struggle for Independence was not just a political struggle but an all-encompassing experience which touched all sensitive individuals irrespective of their religious faiths and cultural upbringing. The tragedy of Partition has few parallels in human history. But Kesavan's book fails to let us enter into the magic of the period and reconstruct the prevailing psychology of the people who witnessed and were affected by those momentous events.

Psychologists tell us that a traumatized mind, a wounded civilization, needs to come to terms with its grief. It attempts to catharize itself with the sublimating works of art and the liberating flights of imagination. The Jewish imagination is still trying to grapple with the Holocaust; the British still looks back to the Raj as much for nostalgia as for exculpation. Khushwant Singh's *Train to Pakistan* is born of 'a sense of guilt'[23] that weighs heavily on the conscience of individuals as well as of the community. But no such guilt weighs on the conscience of Kesavan's protagonist. In the face of the worst famine in the recorded history of India, he says: "Guilt was presumptuous. When I hadn't been able to take one troublesome girl off Haasan's hands, it was silly of me to fret about the live million famine dead of history books." (184) This explains his lack of concern about the victims of Calcutta riots or those who died in Noakhali and West Punjab. The Partition carnage merits only a few sentences in the whole book:

> I dreamt in large clichés: acres of coffins, forests of pyres, rivers of blood skulls. None of this bothered me still a night in June, when one of a heap of skulls showed Masroor's likeness. I pissed in my bed that night. (350)

In *Shame*, Rushdie admits that he is writing a fairy tale about a fictional country which may or may not have similarities with Pakistan. 'Realism,' he says, 'can break a writer's heart.'[24] Similarly, the characters of *Looking through Glass* were 'sceptical about the relevance of real life' and they 'wanted no dealings with reality.' (18) Hence the fantasy, the cock and bull story which Kesavan weaves around history, not to illuminate it. He offers a version of history which is prejudiced, revisionist and even, in its critique of the ideas of change, reactionary. He looks at a hard-earned epoch through a tainted glass. It is not surprising, therefore, that this novel aspired for the Booker. It is the only prize that this book deserves. The British will really appreciate this revisionist project.

NOTES

1. *Imaginary Homelands: Essays and Criticism 1981-1991* (London: Graffiti Books, 1991), pp. 87-101.
2. Rukun Advani, 'Academics as Writers,' *Indian Review of Books*, Vol. 4, No. 1, Oct.-Dec. 1994, p. 3.
3. *Ibid.*
4. Sanjay Iyer, 'Midnight's Grandchildren,' *Indian Review of Books*, Vol. 4, No. 7, May-June 1995.
5. See the blurb.
6. *Freedom at Midnight* (New Delhi: Tarang Paperbacks, 1976), p. 317.
7. Rukun Advani, p. 3.
8. Mukul Kesavan, *Looking through Glass* (New Delhi, Ravi Dayal Publisher, 1995).
9. 'Under the Magnifying Glass,' Kesavan's interview with Pankaj Mishra, *Indian Review of Books*, Vol. 4, No. 7, May-June 1995.
10. Alok Bhalla, *Stories about the Partition of India* (New Delhi: Indus, 1994), p. vii.
11. Salman Rushdie: *Midnight's Children* (London: Picador, 1982), p. 9.
12. *Ibid.*, p. 166.
13. (O.U.P., 1992), p. 124.
14. *Salman Rushdie and the Third World: Myth of the Nation* (New York: St. Martin's Press, 1989), p. viii.
15. Ron Shepherd, '*Midnight's Children* as Fantasy,' *The Commonwealth Review*, Vol. 1, No. 2, 1990, p. 33.
16. Kesavan admits in his interview with Pankaj Mishra that parts of *Looking through Glass* are based on real life incidents, and that 'Dadi is modelled on [his] grandmother.'

17. Sanjay Iyer, 'Midnight's Grandchildren.'
18. *Ibid.*
19. In his brilliantly researched book, *Quit India Revolution: The Ethos of Its Central Direction* (Mumbai: Popular Prakashan), K.K. Chaudhuri asserts that Muslims not only supported but suffered imprisonment during the Quit India Movement. Even the Jamiat-Ul-Ulema-i-Hind positively supported the Congress Campaign. The only people who betrayed the national cause by sabotaging the movement and heaping abuse on the national leaders were the Indian Communists. They became avid collaborators of British imperialism to protect their fatherland, Russia.
20. Larry Collins and Dominique Lapierre, *Freedom at Midnight*, p. 302.
21. Vol. 4, No. 7, May-June, 1995.
22. *Midnight's Children*, p. 435.
23. Khushwant Singh, "Compulsions to Write," *Explorations in Modern Indo-English Fiction*, ed. R.K. Dhawan (New Delhi: Bahri, 1982), p. 185.
24. Salman Rushdie, *Shame* (New Delhi: Rupa, 1983), p. 70.

Woman and Social Class: A Critical Study of Roopa Bajwa's *The Sari Shop*

SARABJIT K.
Guru Nanak Girls College, Ludhiana

Feminist enterprise has been so far a long struggle to universalize female behaviour, focussing common tales of woe and sufferings under realms of patriarchy and male oppression. Be it a question of rewriting of male texts or parametering of social structure, the set pattern of feminist viewpoint has been struggle against androcentric ethics and female sensitivity in bonding, analyzing and understanding each other universally. Nowhere have women been set against women; only men have been peeled, chopped and even roasted in certain instances.

In Indian context, the fashion in writing and criticism pertains to this noveau feminism in vocal, visual and literary form. Roopa Bajwa, the young girl from Amritsar and brave I must say, has dared set in a different viewpoint with her text, *The Sari Shop*. The title itself is a potent symbol of Indian womanhood and all traditional and modern idiosyncrasies associated with it. This is Roopa Bajwa's debut work, and she bangs in a time when Jhumpa Lahiri, Shani Motoo, Anita Nair and other young brigade is all over the scene. But she has a different identity of a small town like Amritsar, an image like Sari to unfurl, and a separate story than an immigrant culture tale, and another woman to portray an Indian woman, a wounded woman, a raped woman, a woman who dares against women, woman who assumes the status of an actual heroine/ role model when she pulls down glitters from fabrics of rich and suave feminist minds by poking fun at their miserableness of being hollow inside. Bajwa has presented in all its nakedness the common psychic inheritance of Indians regarding women and the psychic makeup of women in general.

The continuous assessment all over the world has been of women as important as men but there has been no evaluation of women's position in society with other women. The enigma of plural societies like India, which face more social, political and cultural cleavages, is complex and uneasy to differentiate.

The feminization of media especially T.V. has brought a new cult of upper middle class bourgeois woman, obliterating our minds of the crude statistics of women facing unto untouchability, oppression, below poverty line (bpl status), unemployment graphs, illiteracy or ignorance factors, rising suicides, molestation, violence, rape etc. The embellished make-believe world has bypassed our awareness of internal and external social system in terms of caste, creed, race, colour, ethnicity and religion. Though class in Indian context is not a new signifier, but is the Indian writer in English especially woman writer aware of interclass struggle, class division, class oppression, class-consciousness and class solidarity among women themselves? The uniformity of biological status among women can't ignore rational, social, political and economic differences, where she is a different class from the other. So, there are 'fault lines' emerging among perceived feminist notions and theories, the fancied 'equality manifesto' not with men but with women in general seems itself 'unequal' in theory and reality. *The Sari Shop* is a work where representations of different Indian women is given due analyses on the basis of numerous hybrid and heterogeneous class groups. The rationalization of status and class adds to discrimination between men and women and is discussed in terms of dominant and subordinate category. Frank Parkin has observed in the book *Sociology of Gender*:

> For the great majority of women the allocation of social and economic rewards is determined primarily by the position of their families and, in particular, that of the male head. Although women today share certain status attributes in common, simply by virtue of their sex, their claims over resources are not primarily determined by their own occupation but, more commonly, by that of their fa-

> thers or husbands. And if the wives and daughters of unskilled labourers have something in common with the wives and daughters of wealthy landowners, there can be no doubt that the differences in their overall situation are far more striking and significant. Only if the disabilities attached to female status were felt to be so great as to override differences of a class kind would it be realistic to regard sex as an important dimension of stratification." (Parkin, 1971, 14-15)

The delineated female characters in *The Sari Shop* are better halves of someone rich and famous or somebody affluent and known. They are no entities in themselves. The novelist has called them all Mrs. Sachdeva/ Kapoor/ Bhandari/ Gupta. They have no name and identity of their own. It is all borrowed from husband's hierarchy and tradition. The feminist concern should embark on this hired 'image-identity bargain' of upper-upper class woman. For Kamla, the drunk, mad, ruffian sari assistant Chander's wife, the title is not Mrs. Chander anywhere but Chander's wife or that charred Kamla, 'the mad woman in the attic' kind.

Bajwa introduces a gallery of female characters, all distinct and apart in style, language, mannerism, ideology and in particular how they choose a sari, admire its texture, colour and fabric and fancy it wearing them. Mrs. Sandhu, wife of a chief engineer in Punjab State Electricity Board, epitomizes 'power psychology' "as her rolls of fat jiggled as she waddled" into her spotless house, furnished with latest gadgetry and fashionable architectural feature. Her picture-perfect frame is summed up as "A beautiful house, status family, a caring husband and good looks . . . what more could a woman ask for." (13)

Mrs. Gupta, the wife of a wealthy industrialist sits in her bedroom on a large bed covered with a peach satin bedspread, reminding of the "burnished throne" (A Game of Chess, *The Waste Land*, T.S. Eliot). Her unusual, 'perky' and 'over-confident manner' smelled through her room beaming of various loreal cosmetics, lakme, and her recent venture with feng shui, establishes her as another consumerist character.

Mrs. Sachdeva, Head of the English Department at a local college, "liked to look plain and businesslike." She felt she "wasn't one of the idle housewives that this city was so full of. She was a "literate woman" after all.

Mrs. Bhandari, wife of the DIG of Police, who took pride in calling herself a 'social activist,' 'spoke perfect English, had an unerring taste in clothes and any party that she organized was bound to be a success.' was another straw brilliantly sketched by Bajwa.

And then rich Ravinder Kapoor's wife and daughter, who had, at one go, bought pashmeena shawls worth 10 lakhs, had enough of money and poise to astonish any millionaire in the town.

The personal likings and dislikings of women also rest on these social gimmicks. Mrs. Kapoor dislikes Mrs. Sachdeva, the 'ordinary professor-type service class' women, coming to their mansioned house. Mrs. Sandhu finds Mrs. Bhandari 'snooty,' maybe because 'her English is so good,' but her heaven of peace lies in the fact that 'Bhandaris are certainly not very rich and have only daughter still not married.'

The social nature of women is exposed in the eyes of Ramchand at times by the narrator, sufferer and omniscient observer with critical eye of a psychologist who peeps into their minds, hypocrisies, values and life style for "he had watched innumerable women choose saris. He had seen variety, he had seen envy, he had seen despair. He knew well the bitterness of a plain woman wordless triumph of the beautiful ones." (63)

He finds in Mrs. Kapoor "a certain ruthlessness in the way she picked up a sari, ran a sharp eye a sharp eye, over it and had glint in eyes before making up mind." Among the various sari images created by the author, the imagery used in describing women of different classes picking up the right sari is amazing to see. And in all the cases, Ramchand is made to observe and feel the things, sometimes with Prufrockian uneasiness and sometimes with moralizing of Tiresias.

Mrs. Sachdeva, the literate woman, Head of an English Department, likes dull colours in choosing a sari, symbolic of her argument to stay apart from homogenization with other females. The gorgeously decked up Rina Kapoor as bride dazzles Ramchand with her laughter the way she sweeps the marble staircase regally with her bridal outfit leaves him spellbound.

The sari imagery reflects both beauty and ugliness of life, real and reel. The 'rust red, blood red stains on Kamla's purple sari' and vomit stains on her blouse after her rape and violence become a profound motive for Ramchand to avenge her wrong. The sari image is convulsed, decontrolled and deconstructed with masterly superbness and intensity of pathos. After Kamla's death, the place inside the sari shop turned claustrophobic and grave, saris flew out at Ramchand whipping around 'engulfing him like a shroud,' its black border suffocating him as if coercing him to take stock of situation and bear the burden of a saviour, a role which nature had imposed on him.

Marxist/ socialist feminism rests on the creed of woman as tertiary consumer and primary producer in society, be it producing offspring in the womb or cooking and cleaning or reproducing and writing. The theorization and over-theorization has destabilized the whole system of study and epistemology, regarding women. The debate has rested more on patriarchy in every form and subordination of woman by it. Women's rights, demands and desires have reverberated all the corners by now. Rape, violence, prejudice and household inequities have become highly contested issues among women on behalf of women. The cumulative effect of publicizing deficiency in social system for deprived women by affluent and economic advancement by few has generated a 'cultural lag'[1] between the two, in which the basic values are eroded or changed for two groups and practically even in the name of feminism no cultural and intellectual intermixing is viable.

I see this onslaught of global capitalist consumerist culture on Indian scene in the light of Roopa Bajwa's *The Sari Shop*, which is a fine mimicking of welfare feminism. The class solidarity among opulent group of Mrs. Sandhu, Mrs. Sachdeva, Mrs. Kapoor types is empowered by class consciousness which they feel and generate by ignominious and condescending values to 'have nots.' *The Sari Shop* explains the meaning of existence in spheres of capitalism, chaos and conflict, when women themselves have fallen a prey to consumerism. In the words of Ramchand, the shop assistant: "Life was grubby, clumsy, mean, flabby and meaningless. . . . Sick, sick, sick," (111) enough to remind Burning Burning Burning Burning of Eliot's *The Waste Land*.

The sari of Indian woman is exploited maximum as a potent metaphor, a vehicle for all kinds of feminine expression. Sari is a symbol of womanhood and courtesy, but it also constrains women's movements and gait, providing a negative implication of concept and *The Sari Shop* would be a fit and plausible metaphor of restricted and reserved life, compartmentalized thoughts, associated with various women groups, a fine camouflage behind which all the actual selves remain mystified. Hordes of women visited it daily, some as a part of routine activity which ended in cheap shopping bout at the sari shop, some for weddings and parties, some need not visit, they could pedal saris; some like Kapoors or some occasional visits by sombre lecturers like Mrs. Sachdeva etc. The idiosyncrasies and oddities of women in choosing a sari or touching it brings out their common shared shopping idiocy. The pervading tone of buying, bargaining and spending induces a bizarre sentiment of meaninglessness in life, which Ramchand feels as "Money. Congestion and noise danced an eternal, crazy dance here together, leaving no moving space for other gentler things." (5)

The remarkable thing is why only Ramchand, the traditionally unfair male protagonist, is forced into the situation, to save, revolt and protest moved by helplessness and misery of the rape victim. For it is Ramchand who instead of getting numbed by social pressure and worldliness remarks, "What constant injustice! What a warped way of living! How wrong it all was! He felt reckless, strong enough to do anything, fight anyone for justice, for truth." (222)

Ramchand chooses to narrate Kamla's story for 'more importantly they were women' are enraged by 'the whole ugly, sordid, jigsaw story.' This breakdown of gynocentric world in which women can't live in perfect harmony and friendship with each other for their double standards or sub-standards is alarming! Mrs. Sachdeva pushes away the Saris on her lap and speaks with clenched teeth, "I don't want to listen to all that rubbish again that too in Hindi. . . . How dare you . . . tell me filthy stories about the kind of women you seem to know." Thus, women overdo and cut each other to size, especially the pearl-faced, upper-upper intelligentsia who find bonding with women of their class only, and not with women of Ramchand's social class type.

The gynocentric view is made complete by shooting arrows not only in the direction of men, but also women who are mimicked for their false Anglo-rational feminist ideals, adored and adopted so naturally only to turn deaf to the cries of a marginalized soul for help. A woman is oppressed by women for their tacit understanding of not understanding her plight. Kamla is belied, betrayed and berated by class of her own sex whereas a lone male cries for her existence, her voice, emotion and identity.

Kamla, the wronged, robbed, and raped woman, becomes a symbol and prototype of emancipation and individuality, though she says and does things theatrically in a schizophrenic manner, but it is the will of weaker woman, which overrules the high-handedness of society ladies. The quagmire of assaults she bears throws a neon light on abyss of women's agony at the hands of women, envisioning true feminists to embark on a revolutionary struggle in terms of class conflict among women. Thus a better study lies in giving micro attention to axis of social constructs intertwined with gender and synthesizing feminist dogmas with socio-cultural dimensions.

Works Cited

Bajwa, Roopa. 2004. *The Sari Shop*. New Delhi: Penguin.

Khushwant Singh, 2004. This Above All. *The Tribune*.

Lodge and Wood. 2003. *Modern Criticism & Theory*. Pearson Education.

Rege, Sharmila. 2003. *Sociology of Gender*. New Delhi: Sage.

Image of India in Rohinton Mistry's *A Fine Balance* and Salman Rushdie's *Midnight's Children*: A Comparative Study Towards Diasporic Consciousness

SUREKHA DANGWAL
H.N.B. Garhwal University, Srinagar-Garhwal

Though the writer's individual talent should be rooted in the tradition of a particular society and culture, the real strength of the modern literary imagination lies in the individual's response in terms of belongingness, immigration, expatriation, exile and his/her quest for identity. The diasporic experiences of various writers of diaspora are bound to be different from each other. It has been observed that the Indian Diaspora is one of the most varied community. The scope for finding out the contrast is always there as the place of their origin does not bridge the gap between 'home'—the culture of origin and 'world'—the culture of adoption.

Rohinton Mistry's fiction is rooted in the streets of Bombay, the city he left behind for Canada at the age of twenty-three. The imaginary homeland becomes the literary capital for almost all the Indian Diasporic writers. This image of Bombay has inevitably led to comparison of Rohinton Mistry with Salman Rushdie another Bombay born author settled abroad. However, the differences between these two authors are as compelling as their similarities. Rushdie's *Midnight's Children* and Mistry's *A Fine Balance*, both of which are set in Bombay during the administration of Indira Gandhi and state of internal emergency.

In the present study, these two authors are compared on the basis of their different adopted lands leading to different diasporic consciousness. Even their view and attitude towards their homeland is forced to be different as Rushdie's novel centred around Muslim middle classe while Mistry seems more at home among the Parsi community. Beyond such differences, however, there are certain similarities between these two novels. Both the novels have a tendency to collapse the distinctions between public and private worlds. The present study will certainly be helpful in order to understand and analyze Rohinton Mistry's diasporic consciousness as a prominent writer of South Asian Diaspora.

The word 'diaspora' means the dispersion of the Jews among the Gentiles after the period of their exile. Nearly every Indian writer—or writer of Indian origin writing in English—seems to have decided that the object of his or her imagination has to be the mother country. Jasbir Jain rightly points out that diaspora has the "ambiguous status of being both an ambassador and a refugee." (11) The dilemma between the two is the struggle of diasporic writer. They do not bother about the geographic borders of the nation state, rather the cultural borders perceived by most diasporic writers are quite understandably drawn along national lines. In a world without nation-states, these writers would have merged with others who deal with cultural confrontations of all kinds. But diaspora literature focuses on cultural states that are defined by immigration counters and stamps on one's passport. The diasporic community in world literature is quite varied and complex. It has shown a great mobility and adaptability as it has often been involved in a double act of migration from India to West Indies and from there to Africa and then to Europe or America in search of stability.

To deal with this kind of double triple diaspora, the meetings of disparate cultures occur on various geographic levels: village-city, city-city and country-country. For the writers of 'diaspora literature' however, cultural rendezvous are restricted to those between countries. This is because the authors are themselves dislocated along national lines. The diasporic Indian is "like the banyan tree, the traditional symbol of the Indian way of life, he spreads out his roots in several soils drawing nourishment from one when the rest dry up. Far from being homeless, he has several homes, and that is the only way he has increasingly come to feel at home in the world." (Bhiku Parekh, 106)

The Indian diaspora is varied at its core. The branches of this banyan tree reached far off countries like United States, Canada, Britain, Africa, Caribbean, South America and Australia. The well known among these are V.S. Naipaul, Rohinton Mistry, Bharati Mukherjee, M.G. Vassanji, Salman Rushdie, Amitav Ghosh, Geeta Mehta, Jhumpa Lahiri, Himani Banerji, Suniti Namjoshi, Uma Parmeswaran and Neil Bisoondath. They treat India as their homeland but because of their different adopted lands, their consciousness as a diasporic writer is also different and gets its reflection in their work. But at the same time the Indian diaspora in general has a common concern to have a homeland of one's own.

To analyze a work of art on the basis of different geographic surroundings is no more an important issue because for various historical and economic reasons the postmodern literature has gone global. Any new book from writers like Salman Rushdie, Rohinton Mistry, Bharati Mukherjee, Jhumpa Lahiri and V.S. Naipaul makes a big news. But these diasporic writers continue to be hung up on their national identities even if they do not sometimes admit it to themselves. The odd feature of diasporic literature lies in its continued projection of the writer's motherland, its culture and history. For this specialty the west finds colourful cultural ethnic shades in diasporic writings. Most Indian diasporic writers seem to set their works in India and not in the adopted land. However, in view of the importance of geographical and historical space of any country in which the writer lives, the different consciousness of diasporic literature in terms of adopted land could not be ignored while it is difficult to decide which came first—the consciousness for the surroundings or the natural bent of writing. Writing set in the present setting is more natural. The Indian diaspora writers give expression to difficult voices as per their different immigrant experiences and realities of their new homeland.

Living in diaspora means living in forced or voluntary exile and living in exile usually leads to severe identity confusion and problems of identification with the alienation from the old and new cultures and homelands. Uma Parameswaran observes this making of a Diaspora consciousness in four phases:

> There are four phases of immigrant settlement that are true both at the individual and collective level: the first is one of nostalgia for the homeland left behind mingled with fear in a strange land. The second is a phase in which one is so busy adjusting to the new environment that there is little creative output. The third phase is when immigrants start taking part in the shaping of Diaspora existence by involving themselves in ethno-cultural issues. The fourth is when they have "arrived" and start participating in the larger world of politics and national issues.

However, this obvious development in one's consciousness depends upon the cultures one lives in. The diasporic person is at home neither in the west nor in India and thus 'unhomed' in the most essential sense of the term.

Salman Rushdie and Rohinton Mistry are two diasporic writers having the same origin with two different new homelands. Living in two different alien societies makes their writing fundamentally different even when they are treating the same theme. Rushdie has put the dilemma of diaspora in *Imaginary Homelands* that the position of the exile or immigrant is one of 'profound uncertainties.' To be 'unhomed is not to be homeless' as Homi Bhabha has pointed out in *The Location of Culture*. When the immigrant realizes his homelessness, the world around him confined and squeezed and enlarged slowly afterwards. The unhomely moment of personal and collective consciousness disconnects one's political existence. The personal and collective psychic trauma to the disconnected political existence is clearly evident in the writings of Rohinton Mistry. As Indians who now live and write from Canada and United Kingdom, Rohinton Mistry and Salman Rushdie are the writers of Indian Diaspora. Mistry is a Parsi Zoroastrian and his ancestors were forced into exile by the Islamic conquest of Iran; he was in a diaspora even in India. This kind of multiple displacement is reflected in his writings. His first novel *Such a Long Journey* is prefaced with three epigraphs that evoke a mystical quest motif like that of the Holy Grail. The Parsis' quest for their roots, their past, their heritage is established even before the text itself begins. The first epigraph is from Firdausi's *Shah Nama*, the second from T.S. Eliot's "Journey of the Magi" and the third from Rabindranath Tagore's *Gitanjali*. The lines from the *Shah Nama* recall the Persian imperial past of the Zoroastrian Parsi community to which Mistry belongs. The two other quotations concentrate on the continuous journey that is dominant in the identity crisis of diasporic consciousness. On the other hand Salman Rushdie belongs to Muslim community of India and was born on 20 June 1947, two months before India got independence. This dilemma of being born in the midnight always shows his inclination towards Pakistan and obvious reluctance for India's secular fibre. His choice for his new homeland, Britain, also seems quite obvious.

> I grew up with an intimate knowledge of, and even a sense of friendship with, a certain kind of England; a dream England. . . . I wanted to come to England. I couldn't wait. And to be fair, England has done all right by me. (*Imaginary Homelands*, 18)

In view of the writings of these two diasporic writers and their different diasporic consciousness, the two novels *A Fine Balance* of Rohinton Mistry and *Midnight's Children* of Salman Rushdie have been taken up for analysis in the present study. India is viewed differently by them. The image of India has different shades and colours in the two novels. This paper aims to looking closely at these two novels to discover the image of India in the mind of two diasporic writers who have opted for two different new homelands.

Rushdie's Booker Prize winning book *Midnight's Children* and Mistry's *A Fine Balance* deal with the same central theme—the Emergency excesses of Indira Gandhi. The Emergency saw the suspension of the basic fundamental rights guaranteed to every Indian citizen by the constitution of India. It was first to crush the opposition. Opposition and criticism is what all democratic governments have to contend with and crushing them means jeopardizing the very foundations of democracy. This is exactly what happened during the Emergency and for the very first time since India had been decolonized in 1947, democratic institutions were suspended; what followed was one of the most inglorious chapters in independent India's history. Mistry's *A Fine Balance* records this dark and shameful episode with unrelenting honesty. In an interview soon after the publication of this novel, Mistry says:

> It seemed to me that 1975, the year of the Emergency would be the next important year, if one was preparing a list of important dates in Indian History. And so it was 1975. (Gokhale, October 27, 1996)

Both the novels open with a reference to Bombay. The first few lines of *Midnight's Children* make the intention of the writer clear:

> I was born in the city of Bombay . . . once upon a time. No, that won't do, there's no getting away from the date: I was born in Doctor Narlikar's Nursing Home on August 15th, 1947. And the time? The time matters, too. . . . On the stroke of midnight, as a matter of fact. Clock hands joined palms in respectful greeting as I came. Oh, spell it out spell it out: at the precise instant of India's arrival at Independence. (9)

A Fine Balance is also a text in which Mistry has made a conscious effort to embrace more of the social reality of India. Although the novel opens with a Parsi woman Dina Dalal's story in Bombay. It soon enlarges its scope to include her lodger Maneck Kholah from a hill station in North India and her tailors, Ishwar and Omprakash, who came to her from a village. The primary setting is Bombay 'the dream city' under the Emergency Rule of 1975-77. In a flashback the narration moves to faraway villages and towns before, during and after Partition. The focus is on the Parsi community and the novel is considerably infected with what Saleem Sinai in the other great novel of the emergency calls "an Indian disease, this urge to encapsulate the whole of reality." (94) As the novel *A Fine Balance* centres on the four major characters; two middle-class Parsis and two Hindu untouchables, in *Midnight's Children* the hero Saleem Sinai is from minority community. Apart from Parsi and Muslim community's major characters, scores of minor and middle characters comprise a varied social spectrum of mini India in both the novels: the Muslim rent-collectors and tailors, doctors, lawyer, beggars, murderous strongmen, corrupt slumlords, police, radical students and above all the dominating appearances of Indira Gandhi herself.

Midnight's Children is built almost entirely on such episodes from the fall of the British Empire to that of Indira Gandhi's Emergency rule in India. The beauty of the narration and the presentation of these events in the book is marvelous: either it is the death of Mian Abdullah the Hummingbird or Dr. Narlikar's death in mob violence. Apart from Bombay, the cities like Srinagar, Amritsar, Delhi, Karachi, Dhaka and others make their appearance in the most dynamic manner. The image of India is depicted in its social and political reality. Saleem Sinai remembers not only the Bombay of his childhood but is even able to comment on each and every event that is socially, politically and culturally relevant. He can comment on the state's Reorganization Committee that submitted its report of Nehru in October 1955. India had been divided anew, into fourteen states and six centrally administered territories. But after independence Saleem feels that "language divided us: Kerala was for speakers of Malayalam . . . in Karnataka you were supposed to speak Kanarere." (225) He also remembers the elections of 1957. Murder, politics, elections, businessmen are all presented in the life-size manner. India becomes the central stage and all major and minor characters appear and disappear in order to make a real social and political collage of India. The description of the city Bombay is in fact the 'imaginary homeland' of Rushdie. With the progress of the story, we see the progress of the Indian struggle for independence.

The history of India from 1919 to 1947 is thus encapsulated, here in the form of the first book, out of the three books. The next book narrates the steady progress of Saleem Sinai, the bastard child of a Hindu mother and a British father. That speaks about the Indian history also. Politics, economy and society in India can be said to have had the similar progress. The language riots, the rising threat of communism to the congress party, the deteriorating influence of congress, trials, elections, films, all of them find their way into the pages of the novel. But the writer leaves India and travels along with the members of the family to Karachi. The war between India and Pakistan takes place. Saleem Sinai is the most miserable victim. He has to discontinue his favourite job of eve-teasing and women-hunting. He loses his consciousness because of an Indian air-raid on Karachi. He comes back to consciousness to realize that the sole purpose of the war was to destroy his family completely. He says, "one by one the war eliminated my drained, hopeless family from earth." (411) Book third of the novel is a totally different book. It seems not a part of the main novel *Midnight's Children*. In the first two parts, despite many difficulties and hurdles the growth of Indian democracy is shown but the last part shows the ugly side for Indian democracy. Development is no more a priority of Mrs. Indira Gandhi. Nehru and Shastri become irrelevant. "India is Indira and Indira is India." The Bangladesh war takes place. Saleem Sinai by this time is completely a sub-human creature. He is a leader of a canine unit. His extraordinary telepathic progress is replaced by olfactory sense. The Pakistani government is clever enough to 'utilize' these talents in Saleem Sinai in order to find out and smell out Sheikh Mujibur Rahman. Saleem has forgotten everything about his past, including his name. He is called the "Buddha" because he has calm and quietness on his facial expression. He does his job sincerely. But he misses his way on the Bay of Bengal and enters into Sunderban delta. A strange and wonderful event takes place. A snake bites him and he comes to his senses. This is like any other Bombay Hindi film. Suddenly he realizes his duty and whereabouts. He returns to Dhaka. He sees the arrival of the Indian soldiers, accompanied by a musical band and magicians. Parvati-the-witch, one of the *Midnight's Children*, recognizes him and she takes him along with her back to Delhi hidden in her magic basket.

Now the ugly and dirty side of Indian politics is shown by Rushdie. Saleem is back, again to India. The scene is shifted to Delhi's slums. Like Bombay, Delhi is not the "imaginary homeland" of Rushdie. It is a political slum for him. Saleem's marriage with Parvati-the-witch takes place. Mrs. Indira Gandhi has learned about the children with miraculous gifts. She orders the arrest of all of them. Saleem is first to be arrested and because of the torture of police he gives the list of remaining 580 children as out of 1001 children, 420 were dead earlier because of diseases, famines, strikes and all other disasters. All of them are taken to tubectomy-sections and made impotent. Parvati-the-witch thinks it an honour to visit Shiva, the war hero, secretly and thus to conceive a child during emergency. But even that isolated life of poverty and misery in the slums is thought to be a luxury by Sanjay Gandhi and he is jealous of those slum-dwellers. The road-rollers, tractors and the bulldozers level the slums with the ground. Again Saleem turns to his 'imaginary homeland' Bombay. He is not alone here; from Delhi he has taken with him his son Ganesh—born of Shiva, the war hero and Parvati-the-witch. Parvati dies while giving birth to a child. Ganesh does not speak. In Bombay, he has a good company of Padma, his co-worker. She finds in Saleem a hope for her sexual desire. Saleem warns her that he is foreseeing a total disintegration of his body before his thirty-first birthday. Even his warning cannot stop her from marrying him.

Thus this natural and unnatural ending gives a kaleidoscopic picture of real India with its ups and downs. Indian customs, films, mythology, politics, religion, slums, birth/ marriage/ death ceremonies, friendship, India from Kashmir to Bombay and the pre-partition India from Karachi to Dacca with its variety of situations and shades are shown in the novel.

The main thematic fibre of *Midnight's Children* and *A Fine Balance* is almost same. The treatment of their homeland i.e. India is the original area to provide the big social spectrum of the country. The street performer Monkey-man, whose feat of balancing children atop tall poles provides the cover page of *A Fine Balance* provides the images of India that always being sold to west; the land of magic and snake charmers. Mistry's depiction of Emergency turned "everything upside-down. Black can be made white, day turned into night." (372) Goondas, police, family planning, oppressors and injustice are prominently got expression in the novel. The ugly side of Indian countryside is also shown effectively. Here the age-old caste oppressions continue to flourish, though his knowledge about Indian rural life is always in doubt. The experience is second hand. Still Mistry succeeds to maintain a fine balance. It is this fine balance that if the persons concerned learn to master, helps them to lead a relatively peaceful happy life. If they fail, their life takes a U-turn. Dina as a young girl, a married woman and a dependent widow, constantly upsets the balance of patriarchy and has to pay for it in her truncated education, her husband's death, the loss of her tailors, her home and ultimately her much prized independence. Dina however is a fighter and after every loss of balance, she clambers onto the knife-edge again to once more achieve that ever-elusive fine balance. Maneck too has to learn how to 'balance' between the love of his parents, their mountain home and his need for independence. His sensitive nature fails to achieve a balance between a serene inner life and the outward turmoil of life in the city and has to pay for it with his life. Ishvar and Om have to balance between their own caste origins and their new darji status. There is also a fine balance in the life of nations and the Indian nation had lost that fine balance during the Emergency. But Indian democracy had compelled Mrs. Gandhi to call for fresh elections in which she and her party had been thrown out of office. The fine balance had been restored ultimately.

What makes Rohinton Mistry different from Rushdie is perhaps his ability to draw the reader into Emergency time of crisis. It permits us to feel the horrors and holocaust of it. Certainly, both the novels have many interesting parallels. The social and historical documentation of India, the image of Bombay as a city of social reality, the Bombayya language and the prophetic comprehensiveness. With the abstract symbols of partition, the literal meaning of Indian history become clearer in Mistry. Rushdie's novel is less directly involving, rather his description of partition, India-Pakistan wars and Emergency seemed indirect and translated by the narrator from some history book. Sometimes the novel looks like a scattered and fragmented bundle of dazzling performances rather than collection of lives. Rushdie succeeded in sensitizing the political event like Emergency in *Midnight's Children* but Mistry's *A Fine Balance* is no less politically charged. It is as engrossing and moving as any other good novel on Indian historical heritage. Everything good or bad finds its due place in both the novels. India is like this and we have to accept it.

Works Cited

Homi Bhabha, *The Location of Culture* (London and New York: Routledge, 1994).

Jasbir Jain, ed., *Writers of the Indian Diaspora* (Jaipur and New Delhi: 1998).

Rohinton Mistry, *Such a Long Journey* (Toronto: McClelland and Stewart, 1991).

_____. *A Fine Balance* (Toronto: McClelland and Stewart, 1995).

Bhiku Parekh, "Some Reflections on the Indian Diaspora," *Journal of Contemporary Thought*, Baroda: 1993.

Uma Parameswaran, "Writing the Diaspora," *The Atlantic Literary Review*, Vol. 1, 2, 2000.

Salman Rushdie, *Midnight's Children* (Jonathan Cape, London 1991).

_____. *Imaginary Homelands* (London: Granta Books, 1992).

Culture-Consciousness and Gender Bias in Bapsi Sidhwa's *The Pakistani Bride*: A Postcolonial Approach

DIPIKA SAHAI
D.A.V. College, Kanpur

Today the most vital writing in English comes from Britain's former colonies in the so-called third world. There has been a geographical explosion of literature in English. After the partition and decolonization of the Indian subcontinent in 1947, the writings in English split up into distinct national canons. Writings in India, Pakistan and Sri Lanka have diverged from each other because of their different cultures and identities. Re-distribution of the subcontinent into sovereign postcolonial states had its effect on literary cultures, giving place to national traditions, geography and history, multi-lingual and multi-ethnic socio-economic order, politics and aesthetics. For many writers in Pakistan, as Vinay Dharwadker has observed, the search for a distinctive national identity has led to a "new literary archeology."[1] The writers have "directed their verbal excavations at Pakistan's rugged landscape, which changes rapidly from icy mountain and fertile river valley to desert and seashore."[2] Literature becomes a vehicle for indigenous expression. The writers in postcolonial era focus on ethnic identities rather than racial divisions, male dominance rather than European colonization.

Bapsi Sidhwa is the author of four internationally acclaimed novels, and is one of Pakistan's most prominent English fiction writers. She was born in Karachi and brought up in Lahore. She now divides her time between U.S.A. where she teaches creative writing and Pakistan. In Pakistan she is an energetic advocate of improved social and legal conditions for women. She represented Pakistan at the Asian Women's Conference in 1975. As a member of the relatively small Parsi community in Pakistan, she is conscious of the problems of insecurity and insularity faced by minority communities everywhere. In 1978, at a time when publishing in English was practically non-existent in Pakistan, Sidhwa published her novel *The Crow Eaters*. It was published in Britain in 1980, a year before Rushdie's *Midnight's Children*. It was the first major novel about Parsis. While *The Pakistani Bride*, also published as *The Bride* in 1982, was the first novel Sidhwa wrote, it was the second to be published. *Ice-Candy-Man*, also published as *Cracking India*, is her third novel for which she has been awarded the Literature Prize in Germany. *An American Brat*, Sidhwa's latest book, was published in 1993.

The Pakistani Bride deals with the lives of another culturally and geographically remote group, the inhabitants of Pakistan's harsh mountainous regions. Pakistan's population is mostly Muslim, yet beneath this religious unity there is cultural diversity in different regions, especially between the plains and the mountains. *The Pakistani Bride* is a work of fiction based on the events from a tribal girl's life. Bapsi Sidhwa was on a visit to Karakoram mountain area of Pakistan with her husband where the tragic story of a young girl brought to the tribal areas as a bride was narrated to her. The girl, unable to bear the tortures inflicted on her, had run away, but was murdered on being found because she had brought dishonour and disgrace to the tribe. Sidhwa was so touched by the story that it haunted her when she came back to Lahore. She began her writing career at the age of twenty-six. She wanted to write the girl's story and also about the poor tribals and their pride in their valour and honour. Sidhwa sat down to write a short story which turned into her first novel *The Bride*.

The poetic imagination of Sidhwa named the girl in the novel, Zaitoon, who became an orphan during the Partition riots. She is adopted by Qasim, a Kohistani who had to leave the mountains and was on his way to Lahore from Jullundur. Qasim was a lonely man after the death of his wife and children because of small pox. He is touched when a girl of five whose parents are dead, sobs and calls him "Abba, Abba, my Abba."[3] (29) In her face he sees the face of his daughter lost long ago. Hence he gives her the same name: "Munni, you are like the smooth dark olive . . . the zaitoon that grows near our hills. . . The name suits you. . . . I shall call you Zaitoon." (30) He makes a home for the two of them in the glittering city of Lahore. They have Nikka and Miriam as neighbours, who, too, love Zaitoon as their child. As the years pass by Qasim leads a comfortable life, but is nostalgic about his life in the mountains. Impulsively, he promises Zaitoon in marriage to a man of his tribe in the mountains despite Miriam's caution that Zaitoon will be miserable there. Miriam says: "I tell you, she'll be a slave, you watch, and she'll have no one to turn to, No one!" (93) It turns out to be real. For Zaitoon, brought up in the civilized city atmosphere, the tribal life becomes traumatic. After becoming the wife of Sakhi and the bestial treatment meted out to her, she resolves to run away, though she knew that by the tribal code the punishment for such an act was death, yet she contemplates the ultimate escape—the one from which there is no return.

The concept of Postcoloniality is to give expression to indigenous cultures once subjugated under colonial rule. Postcolonial theory accepts Benedict Anderson's contention that nations are imaginative and cultural artefacts rather than empirical and scientific entities. They are imagined into coherence in spite of their varied cultural identities.[4] In postcolonial literature we find a rejection of colonial hegemony and positional superiority of Western consciousness. Indigenous cultures are given full expression with their historical background, customs and beliefs, irrespective of their being good or bad. Macaulay's statement tried to prove the inferiority of colonized cultures and their literature. This pre-eminence of English writers was challenged by African writers as well as the writers of the Indian subcontinent after gaining Independence.

In *The Pakistani Bride* this culture-consciousness is foremost. As Sidhwa tells us, Qasim was "a simple man from a primitive, warring tribe." (30) Because of his white skin, tall and robust build, he was conspicuous as a mountain-man anywhere in Lahore. He hates to be called a Pathan. He is conscious of his identity and says: "I am not a Pathan, I am Kohistani." (36) He protests at being called a Chinaman by Mustaq: "Is this a Chinaman's nose? No! It leaps forth as a banner of my race! A legacy from Persian ancestors who came through those hills with Cyrus and Darais . . . or from the Yahudis even. . . . Some say the lost tribe of Israel settled here." (132)

When he first arrived in Jullundur from the mountains, Qasim spoke Hindko, a distorted mixture of Punjabi and Pushto. But gradually he became conversant with Punjabi and Urdu. Sidhwa has used words and phrases from the native language. Words like 'chappati,' 'hookah,' 'manja,' 'zenana,' 'payal,' 'chum chum of feminine feet dancing,' 'dancing bulbul' are freely used in the novel. She has also quoted from Iqbal.

Sidhwa has given a vivid description of the distinctive dress of Kohistanis, the sheepskin waistcoats and shirts made from beaten wool. Uncured leather wrapped around their legs, taking on the shape of their calves, resembled knee-length boots. (151) And the mountain diet consisted of flat maize bread soaked in water. These tribals had a "fierce capacity to love or hate, to lavish loyalty or pity. Each emotion arose spontaneously and without complication, and as reinforced by racial tradition, tribal honour and superstition." (30) Qasim says, "Generations had carried it that way in his volatile Kohistani blood." (30)

Different customs, the landscape and the mountains are described by Sidhwa with immense vigour and liveliness and she has brought her world and people exuberantly to life. When Qasim was returning to his people, to the house of his ancestors, the vigorous air and the sight of the stark mountains stirred in him a long dormant pride. "He read the marks of his ancestry in each arrogant face." (151)

He tells Zaitoon: "Bibi, you will like my village. Across the river, beyond those mountains, we are a free and manly lot. . . . You will see how different it is from the plains. We are not bound hand and foot by government clerks and police. We live by our own rules—calling our own destiny! We are free as the air you breathe." (100) We are told that the tribals could be "trigger happy." (116)

There is the other side of their character too. "The Kohistanis are quite untameable," (116) as Sidhwa tells us. They are feuding tribes. "They have their own notions of honour and revenge; a handful of maize stolen, a man's pride slighted, and the price is paid in bloody family feuds." (115)

Mushtaq narrates an incident in which a Khan was paid six thousand rupees in compensation for his land evacuated by the government. He had thought that the Khan would use that money in improving his miserable lot. But to his shock he found that the Khan shot the male members of an entire clan. It led a load off his mind and his conscience at ease. And the next day he pays his fine to the Wali of Swat. "Six thousand rupees, the fine for ten murders!"[8] (11) Something unimaginable. Killing was easy with them. Qasim tells the old man in the train "I killed a baboo just before getting here" (21) because he had ridiculed Qasim. "Death was the price for daring such an insult to his tribe, his blood, his religion." (23)

The difference is in the basic values. Life was easy in plains. To Qasim, "the men of the plains appeared strangely effeminate. . . . Where he came from, men—as in the Stone Age—walked thirty days over the lonely, almost trackless mountains to secure salt for the tribes." (21) It was a tough life. The tribals were "Routed by centuries of ruthless pride, submerged beneath the hard toil, buried in a way of life that could afford no sentiment. . . . [They were] Quick to anger, in a land where pride and wrath are nurtured from boyhood." (171) Like all tribals, the Kohistanis hated the outsiders. This hatred is quite apparent when they talk about Carol, the American woman married to Farukh, the Army officer.

The women artists of Pakistan are grappling every moment of their lives with the problems of gender identity and role. The pressures on women are enormous as Salima Hashmi's book *Unveiling the Visible* shows. In the novel *The Far Thing* (1997) by Mai Kureishi, who, like Sidhwa, is a woman from the tiny minority of Parsis in Pakistan, focuses on gender issues. Individual voices of protest found in Pakistani women poets and novelists in the postcolonial period are poignant. Their rebellion shows the need to challenge outdated traditions and customs. For centuries the very concept of womanhood has forbidden to woman the right to deviate. Women are seen as gender only, and not as human beings.

The Pakistani Bride starts with showing the low status of women in the Kohistani tribe where girls were given in marriage in exchange of loan due. When Qasim's marriage was being settled his father had first thought of marrying the girl himself. Sidhwa writes: "He [Qasim's father] had only one wife; but in twinge of paternal conscience, he decided to bestow the girl on Qasim. It was his first duty." (8)

After the marriage fifteen-year-old Afshan is shocked to see Qasim, a boy of ten as her husband. "The girl didn't know whether to laugh or cry." (10) Gradually she accepted her lot cheerfully. Later on we find Mushtaq, a Major in the Army commenting on marriage: "A wife was a symbol of status, the embodiment of a man's honour and the focus of his role as a provider. A valuable commodity indeed, and dearly bought." (138)

When Ashiq, the jawan, cautions Zaitoon about the murders and family feuds in the hill tribes, Zaitoon's reply is "It is my father's wish. I must go with him!" (144) When the marriage has been solemnized we find Sakhi surveying his bride Zaitoon with "proprietorial lust and pride." (159) As the novel progresses Zaitoon becomes immune to the tyrannical animal-trainer treatment meted out to her by Sakhi. He used to beat her on the slightest pretext. "She no longer thought of marriage with any sense of romance. She now lived only to placate him." (174)

When she is standing by the riverside. Sakhi goes on hitting her with stones until she falls down with deep injuries. That was the night when Zaitoon resolved to run away. She knew that in flight lay her only hope of survival." (186) Then carefully she ventured into the unfamiliar hills. Her struggle for emancipation is full of tragic incidents.

Sidhwa has shown the condition of women through animal imagery which is prominent in the novel. Sakhi is often mentioned as 'hissing.' After meeting Zaitoon, Carol comments: "This girl had no more control over her destiny than a caged animal." (136) Even in dream, Zaitoon could "sense the savagery of the people." Tribals take guns not to search the girl, but to hunt her. Mushtaq tells Carol about the run-away girl: "The girls run away. The whole bloody clan's out hunting her." Carol is surprised and asks: "Hunting her? What will they do when they find her?" Mushtaq replies, "Beat her up. Probably kill her." (223)

We are told that women get killed for one reason or other—imagined insults, family honour, infidelity, Carol is aghast to know that in the region women are killed even for "imagined infidelity." (223) She takes it as an insult to herself and women kind. "That's really what's behind all the gallant and protective behaviour I've loved so much here, isn't it? I felt very special, and all the time it didn't matter to you any more than the girl does as an individual to those tribals, not any more than a bitch in heat. You make me sick. All of you." (224)

Zaitoon's pain and agony after the rape, her licking the bruises like a wounded animal, subsequent wandering in delirium and the hallucinations are more tragic than even Lear's. She realizes: "So, I am to die after all, she thinks . . . her destiny is compressed into seconds. She hurtles in a short-cut through all the wonders and wisdom of a life unlived. Instantly old, her tenure spent, she is ripe to die." (235) At this moment she has an unexpected insight: "She was certain, that in these very moments she had lived through one version of her destiny and that somehow she had escaped it, though at a price. She would remain stamped with its horror. . . She was certain now that Sakhi was near-by, waiting to kill her." (235)

Still she rises above the situation and is ready to pardon him. She thinks: "It is not an act of personal vengeance; he is dispensing justice—the conscience and weight of his race are behind him." (235)

At the end when the Major finds the skeletal creature Zaitoon in the dark hollow between the stones, he wondered if it was the same girl. The girl, in an attempt to cover her nakedness, began to smooth and pull at her torn clothes. Mushtaq felt a surge of pity. He huddled the girl in the blanket and sent it to the Army Mess telling the jawans that it was a bundle of roots, and to Sakhi he informed: "Your wife is dead. Understand me? You have no option. You have to take my word for it. She is dead. . . . The jawans know she is dead. I swear no one will say otherwise. . . . I give you my word. Your honour will not be sullied." (243) For Sakhi, it was "for the first time he faced a humiliation he could not avenge: a sorrow he dared not share." (243) As for his father Misri Khan and brother Yunus Khan: "It was as if a breeze had cleared the poisonous air suffocating them and had wafted an intolerable burden from their shoulders." (244) The Major noticed: "Misri Khan's back straightened. He saw the triumphant swagger in Yunus Khan's gait and Sakhi's relaxed lope as they resumed their journey." (244) They soon disappeared. Their honour was saved. For them the girl was dead.

Mushtaq visualized a new world for Zaitoon. She could either be sent with Carol to Lahore or even to the States or perhaps Ashiq could propose marriage to her once she recovered. But the old Kohistani Qasim must never know she was alive. Sidhwa says that it was a pity that he appeared to love her. Still, he was to be blamed for imposing his will on something that was bound to end in disaster.

Hence we see in the novel how female emotional demands are crushed by violence. Despite Zaitoon's predicament Sidhwa has shown that through struggle there is hope even for women to see the dawn.

The Pakistani Bride is a woman's lyric cry in prose against the existential fate and societal abuse. Sidhwa has fashioned complex metaphors to orchestrate the multiple agonies of a woman, a successful portrayal of pain and suffering in the character of Zaitoon. She has written dramatically of a particular culture, marriage, loyalty, honour and their conflict with old ways. She has introduced the reader to an exotic new world. In an entertaining style she has drawn the reader into Pakistan, the hill areas, the bazaars of Lahore and the native language.

The novel also reveals that in the last few decades women in Pakistan have gained confidence to articulate their thoughts. The change from the European-inspired vocabulary to a bold look at one's own visual culture and appropriation of images and motifs from one's background is an exciting journey for the postcolonial writer.

NOTES

1. Vinay Dharwadker, "Poetry of the Indian Subcontinent," *A Companion to Twentieth Century Poetry*, ed. Neil Roberts (U.K.: Backwell, 2001), p. 275
2. *Ibid.*
3. Bapsi Sidhwa, *The Pakistani Bride* (New Delhi: Penguin, 1990), p. 36.
4. B. Anderson: *Imagined Communities: Reflections on the Origin and Spread of Nationalism* (London: Verso, 1991, 2nd ed.), p. 6

Portrayal of Indian Polity in Girish Karnad's Plays: A Comparative Study of *Tughlaq* and *Tale-Danda*

LAKHWINDER SINGH GILL
S.R. College for Women, Amritsar

To draw present meaning from the past is Girish Karnad's fond occupation. He picks up the relevant material from the events that occurred in the past, shapes and reshapes them as they suit his dramatic purpose. In his hands the story with old subject matter gets new meaning. It is not the subject matter that is old or new, it is the treatment, holds Girish Karnad, that is of crucial importance. If a playwright has modern sensibility the play gets modern, howsoever old its subject matter may be. It is from this perspective that Girish Karnad's *Tughlaq* and *Tale-Danda* are modern plays. Their stories are old but his treatment of them is modern: his modern awareness makes these plays relevant to our times.

Tughlaq and *Tale-Danda* move around historical events. If *Tughlaq* draws its material from the history of India, *Tale-Danda* derives it from a regional incident in the history of Karnataka that took place in the city of Kalyan in the 12th century A.D. Eight hundred years ago; a man called Basavanna assembled a congregation of poets, mystics, social revolutionaries and philosophers. They were unmatched for their creativity and social commitment in the history of Karnataka. They opposed idolatry, rejected idol worship and upheld the equality of sexes and rejected discrimination among human beings on the basis of caste and creed. Events took a violent turn when they brought their belief of casteless society into practice. The movement started for the cause of humanity ended in bloodshed. A prosperous society plunged into anarchy and terror. Karnad's *Tale-Danda* pictures only one week of those turbulent days in Karnataka.

If we take up Karnad's *Tughlaq* first, we see that in the story of a Sultan who ruled India in the 14th century, we find the story of Indian polity after independence. The opening scene in front of the Chief Court of Justice, in India, with a mixture of the Hindus and the Muslims stands for the present Indian society which mainly comprises these two communities. The first sentence, "God, what's this country coming to?"[1] (147) reflects the present scenario where every Indian who is generally religious and has faith in India's rich cultural heritage seems to ask. The drift of the present-day India from its past is a matter of serious concern for everyone. This sentence suggests the widening gap between what India and Indianness was and what it has been reduced to by its rulers. The Indians hated the Britishers and pushed them out because they deprived the Indians of their rights, exploited them, deceived them and finally made them strangers in their own land. But independence, too, brought no substantial change for the common Indian. Rather, the situation deteriorated from bad to worse; the common Indian is being deceived by his own countrymen and there is complete degeneration of human values. The feeling of brotherhood and commonness which stood its ground in the face of foreigners' rule began to vanish soon after independence. So the old man's concern for "what the country is coming to?" is very relevant in this context. His lament is the lament of every Indian when human values have taken back seat: "I don't know. I've been alive a long time, seen many Sultans, but I never thought I would live to see a thing like this." (147)

Muhammad's hypocritical attitude towards religion and the religious practices is identical with the attitude of the political leaders of independent India. They use religion for their political motives. In the opening scene, the Young Man defends Muhammad as being a staunch believer in Islam: "Tell me, how often you prayed before he came to the throne? Not even once a week, I bet. Now you pray five times a day because that's the law and if you break it, you'll have the officers at your neck. Can you mention one earlier Sultan in whose time people read the Koran in the streets like now?" (147) At this, the Old Man rightly points out the futility of such an exercise: "What's the use? One must act according to it." This indeed is a hint at the hollowness of the religious values the Indian rulers advocate. They profess religion but they don't "act" according to it, suggests the playwright.

The communal cracks in the Hindus and the Muslims in Muhammad's regime also speak of the hostility between the two communities in India. The Third Man is critical about the Hindus who are not paying the Jaziya tax which he feels is against the Koran. The all-pervasive nature of Hinduism with which it has absorbed many other small religions is also referred to by the Old Man: "Beware of the Hindu who embraces you. Before you know that, he will turn Islam into another caste and call the Prophet an incarnation of his god." (148) This reflects the inherent fear of Muslims as a minority community. They nurse a feeling that their community can be taken into its fold by the Hinduism. And the final reference to the communal riots in Kanpur is highly suggestive of the current communal violence in various parts of India.

Muhammad, outwardly benevolent but inwardly deceptive, is like the present Indian ruler who carries deep-rooted duality in his character. Muhammad proclaims, "My beloved people, you have seen for oneself how justice works in my kingdom without any consideration of might or weakness of religion or creed." (149) The modern Indian leader similarly plays with the religious feelings of the people. Muhammad's attempt to look a true Muslim King by making five times prayer a must in a day is basically a political device. In fact, he has murdered his own father while he was praying and announced that it was an accident. So prayer has no sanctity for him. Basically, his innerself is that of an atheist. The non-believer in him has put the Sayyids and the Ulema behind the bars. But to the public he proclaims, "I've never denied the word of God. Because it is my bread and my drink." (164) He has the Muslims, the Hindus and the Jains etc. in his country, so he speaks the language which offends none. His approach to religion is purely political. Like an Indian ruler, he has no hesitation to confess, "I have never denied the world of God. Because it is my bread and butter. . . . Only an atheist can try to be God. . . . I am God's most humble slave." (169) After an attempt is made on his life, he bans prayer forever only to revoke it later.

Thus the idea of prayer in the play becomes an image of the idea of religion in general which is used and misused by the rulers to their convenience. Imam-ud-din's advise to Mohammad is, "Religion! Politics! Take heed, one day these verbal distinctions will rip you into two." (165) It is from this angle that a critic observes, "In this powerful play, politics is deftly linked with religion."[2] Using Sheikh Imam-ud-din for his political game by Muhammad epitomizes the use of religion and religious men by the political leaders. Mohammad makes the Sheikh his envoy because he is a Muslim saint and none doubts his integrity. Having understood his crooked design, the Sheikh rightly comments, "I am just going to understand why they say you are the cleverest man in the world?" (167) Later we see that the Sheikh is killed by the soldiers of Muhammad.

Muhammad's dreams of the future are identical with the dreams of India. U.R. Anantha Murthy observes, "It is a play of the Sixties and reflects as perhaps no other play does the political mood of disillusionment which followed the Nehru era of idealism in the country."[3] Muhammad too wants to "build an ideal umpire." (149) His new steps of shifting the capital from Delhi to Daulatabad and change the currency etc. remind of the new experiments introduced in the Independent India. The socio-economic measures in the form of the Five Year Plans, the introduction of democracy through newly framed constitution and many more new national and international policies formulated by its rulers and the inherent contradictions in them carry implicit comment of the playwright. By showing the result of the innovative experiments made by Muhammad, Karnad appears to be apprehensive about the policies and their implementation in the independent India. Muhammad's idealism appears to have a close parallel to the mood of disillusionment which followed Nehru era of idealism. In the words of Girish Karnad, "In a sense, the play reflected this slow disillusionment of my generation felt with the new politics of independent India: the gradual erosion of the ethical norms that had guided the movement of independence, and coming to terms with cynicism and real politic."[4]

However, he denies having made any conscious effort to associate the rule of Muhammad Tughlaq with that of Nehru. He feels that the similarity between the two is "accidental": "I did not consciously write about the Nehru era, I am always flattered when people tell that it was about the Nehru era. . . . But, I think, well, that it is a compliment that any playwright would be thrilled to get, but it was not intended to be a contemporary play about a contemporary situation."[5]

The atmosphere of violence, bloodshed, treachery and corruption from top to the bottom is suggestive of the contemporary social unrest in India. The people of the independent India confronted two major problems: poverty and violence generated by the wrong political policies. If Muhammad's subjects rush from Delhi to Daulatabad with high hopes, then the people of India too had high hopes when they shifted from the British rule to the self-rule. Like them, the Indians too experienced with disappointment and frustration in place of peace and prosperity. In the name of democracy they experienced opportunistic politics leading to communalism and lawlessness all around. It is because of this parallelism that Tejwant S. Gill observes, "No wonder, the life, rule and time of this charismatic and erratic emperor have past significance, the present meaning . . . is getting more and more pronounced with the passage of time."[6]

Mixing up of caste and religion with politics remains a dominant idea in *Tale-Danda* too. The idea of casteism which finds only a casual reference in *Tughlaq*, becomes a major issue in *Tale-Danda*: "The central theme of *Tale-Danda* is that of deconstruction of caste and religion to arrive at its real, proper meaning and to restructuring the same for the benefit of the society and the country."[7]

The Indian society was traditionally divided into four *varnas* (castes) and even the professions of the people were categorized accordingly. Now with the passage of time there is a freedom in the choice of profession but Indians have not been able to liberate themselves mentally from the idea of caste and creed. Rather, caste system remains an integral part of Indian thinking. As such, inter-caste marriages are not a very common phenomenon. *Tale-Danda* exposes this ugly deformity of the Hindu society. In this play, the movement against the social evil is launched by the Sharanas for whom sincerity of action and selfless service of humanity is a true religion in which all human beings are equal. But it does not suit the king Bijjala. As a leader he accepts this new religion only to the extent it serves his political interests. The dual attitude of Bijjala towards the concept of casteless society speaks of his politics oriented approach. In spite of being a Shudra by caste he does not support inter-caste marriage to be arranged by the Sharanas. His attitude to the caste-based division of society is confined to his power politics.

Bijjala's views about the casteless society become obvious when he discusses this issue with his wife Rambhavati. In his conversation with her, he appreciates the cause of the Sharanas. He knows that they want to eradicate caste-system "from the face of the earth, annihilate the Varna system. What a vision! And what prodigious courage!"[8] But when his wife asks him why doesn't he join them too, his answer is: "It'll solve nothing." Quoting the verse of Basavanna, he tells her: "It is not, as you can see, an ethics designed for rulers, worse still is their 'Bhakti' their devotion, their incessant craving for the Lord's grace." (15) Here we also remember the duality in Muhammad's character as a king. Like him, Bijjala feels that a ruler has different ethics to follow. Bijjala too has built temples but not for a spiritual reason, "I've built temples to keep my subjects happy. But the one truth I know is that I exist and God doesn't." (15) He says that he is an ordinary king and he wants "No truck with the gods. I go by the laws of the land, which is why this mass hunger for divine grace bothers me greatly." (23) But he never keeps religion and politics apart and recognizes that Basavanna like Imam-ud-Din in *Tughlaq* has sway over the masses as a religious leader, so he sends him to Maddu to pacify his violent followers.

Bijjala and Basavanna's relationship like that of Mohammad and Sheikh Imam-ud-Din in *Tughlaq* can also be interpreted in the modern sense when religious and social heads are patronized by the rulers for their political gains. Likewise, Bijjala's attitude towards Basavanna is purely politics-oriented. He likes his philosophy so far as it enhances his own interest as a king. But he would not let it grow beyond a limit. He brings Basavanna and his followers to his territory as they are "only to earn the day's keep," "make no extra demand" and "treat profits with contempt." This attitude helps only the king. He confesses, "For their honest labour, trade and commerce have come pouring into Kalyan and now the city is busting with money. Even those who despise the Sharanas for their beliefs need them for their economic enterprise—as indeed I do." (24) So his direct and indirect support to the Sharanas is not without politics in it. He allows them some liberty not because their cause is just but because he needs them.

About the contemporaneity in *Tale-Danda*, Karnad once observed, "when people all-around us are slaughtered in the name of the temple, I hear echoes from those times long past . . . it seems eight hundred years have solved no problem. We are back exactly where we started."[9] Like the communal violence at Kanpur in *Tughlaq*, in *Tale-Danda* too, the Jain temples are being occupied by force. The Sharanas threaten to "smash the naked idols and turn it into a Shiva temple." (28) This is a typical incident that reminds one of the communal violence in India in the name of religion and religious places. In *Tale-Danda* too, the fundamentalists won't let the tribals of Andhra and Gangodho enter their territory on their side of the river because the tribals are from a low-caste. Basavanna appears to be the spokesman of Karnad when he asks the other Sharanas to shun violence in any form. Basavanna's remark in response to Jagadeva's idea is relevant in the Indian context: "Violence is wrong, whatever the provocation. Who resorts to it because someone else started it first is even worse. And to do so in the name of structure of brick and mortar, is a monument of stupidity." (29) These words of

Basavanna reflect the modern Indian socio-political crisis and provide the answer as well:

> The rich
> Will make temples of Shiva
> What shall I,
> A poor man do?
> My legs are pillars
> The body, the Shrine
> The head of cupola
> Of gold . . .
> Things standing shall fall
> But the moving shall ever stay. (29)

These words of Basavanna appear to hint at the root cause of all communal problems in India i.e. we are "standing" and not "moving" and in order to progress we have to move. About the so-called miracles which the Indians are prone to believe in, Basavanna says, "Isn't this life abundant enough? Do we need more miracles?" (29)

The current idea of religious conversion from one religion to another can also be derived from the happenings in *Tale-Danda*. Kalyana and Gundhanna inform Basavanna about the arrival of some tribals in the region. Kalayna suggests to Basavanna about their belief in idol worship and desires that they should be taken in their fold by the Sharanas: "Basavanna, those tribal have brought their god with them. You should see that idol. Rolling eyes, a tongue lolling out. . . . So the sooner they initiate them into their fold the better." (35) But Basavanna's approach is highly realistic. He replies, "A roof over their head first and a piece of land to spread their mats on. We can minister to their spiritual needs later" (35) This view is important in the contemporary context where some communities in India are visualizing a threat to their existence as their people are converting into other communities such as Christianity. But our main interest, at present is to cater to the physical needs of the people and their spiritual concern should be put on a back burner, suggests Girish Karnad. Gangabhika, the wife of Basavanna, offers bags of paddy, textiles, salt and spices for the tribals who are coming from Andhra. The sufferings of these tribes who have tracked for weeks in search of food and shelter and hunger and starvation of the people on their way from Delhi to Daulatabad in *Tughlaq*, remind the sufferings of the poor in India. As Chaman Ahuja says: "his works make telling comments on the general human situation and the specific socio-political goings on in the country today."[10]

Bijjala is also instrumental in striking at the very base of caste system i.e. the men from the higher-castes have born superiority over those of the lower-castes. And the men from the lower-castes lack the ability to rule. Bijjala, the king, is not from any higher caste. He is a barber and still he is full of kingly insight. He is of the view that for kingship heredity is no qualification. He rejects Sovideva as his descendent on the ground that he does not have the qualities of a ruler. He is in complete agreement with Basavanna when he argues, "Kingship is a calling. A source of living, yes, but also a duty and a service of humanity. It is not an inheritance, not a family gift but a right to be earned, to be justified by diligent application." (20) And Bijjala as a king proves that good administration is not a property limited to the higher castes. As a king he knows well what he is to do and what he should not. His approach to the Sharanas is very practical. He accepts and ejects them keeping in view his political interest. He likes Sharanas because they are self-less workers but does not fully encourage them because they can be a potential threat to his power. When Basavanna offers to step down as his treasurer, the king in Bijjala comes out: "If you think I have ascended the throne merely to sit back and scratch my arm you are in for a surprise. . . . You think you can twist my arms behind my back and push me around. . . . I am Bijjala." (40) But the moment he learns that his threat trick has not worked well and Basavanna is not to budge an inch from his stand, he prefers to withdraw, "So be it. Have your wedding. I won't come in the way because I know I can't." (50) Thus, through Basavanna's definition of kingship and Bijjala's capability as a king, the playwright challenges the idea of the division of human beings on the basis of birth that ignores individual merit and capability. In view of this contemporary meaning of the play, Girish Karnad writes in its preface,

> I wrote *Tale-Danda* in 1989 when the Mandir and the Mandal movements were beginning to show how relevant the question posed by these thinkers was for our age. The horror of subsequent events and the religious fanaticism that has gripped our national life today have only proved how dangerous it is to ignore the solutions they offered.

It is from this aspect that a critic says, "*Tale-Danda* is relevant today as religious fundamentalism is strong enough to destroy the Babri Masjid and claim the lives of thousands of people.[11] At the end we can say that both *Tughlaq* and *Tale-Danda* forward profound commentary over the Indian polity after independence. If *Tughlaq* puts a question mark on the political vision of the present Indian ruler and his lack of understanding the nature of the problems being faced by India, *Tale-Danda* brings into focus the caste ridden politics that has marred the Indian polity. A ruler may be from a low or a high caste; he wants to maintain the division of society on the basis of caste as it promotes his interests. Both the plays expose the use of religion for political motives by the Indian ruler: the playwright successfully employs historical events for contemporary purpose.

NOTES

1. Girish Karnad, "Three Plays: *Hayavadana*, *Nagamandala*, *Tughlaq* (New Delhi: Oxford University Press, 1994).
2. P. Bayapa Reddy, "The Theatrical Representation of History: A Study of *Tughlaq*," *The Plays of Girish Karnad: Critical Perspectives*, p. 150.
3. U.R. Anantha Murthy, "Introduction to *Tughlaq*," *Three Plays*, p. 143.
4. *Ibid.*, p. 7.
5. Qtd. R.K. Dhawan, "Girish Karnad: The Man and the Writer," *The Plays of Girish Karnad: Critical Perspectives*, p. 16.
6. Tejwant S. Gill, "*Tughlaq*: Its Past Significance and Present Meaning," *Bharati Journal of Comparative Literature*, Vol. II, No. 1 (1987), pp. 57-58.

7. A.R. Shukla, "Caste and Religion in *Tale-Danda*," *The Plays of Girish Karnad: Critical Perspectives*, p. 290.
8. Girish Kanad, *Tale-Danda* (New Delhi: Paul Press, 1993).
9. "Where is the Tradition?" (Interview), *Frontline*, 25 Sept. 1992, p. 76.
10. Chaman Ahuja, "I am Trying to Create a Tradition of my Own," (Interview), *The Observer*, 24 March 1999.
11. M. Sarat Babu, "Social Deformity in *Tale-Danda*," *The Plays of Girish Karnad: Critical Perspectives*, p. 287.

Mythical Archetypes and Girish Karnad's *The Fire and the Rain*

AWANISH RAI
D.D.U. Gorakhpur University

"In literature, whatever has a shape has a mythical shape, and leads us towards the centre of the order of words."[1] This is how Northrop Frye concludes his argument in his apocalyptic essay "Myth, Fiction and Displacement" where he begins his discussion by dividing literary works broadly in two categories, 'the fictional and the thematic' and resolves to concentrate only upon the former one. He agrees with Aristotle in his concept of plot and its importance and redefines it in a larger perspective by asserting that in a play or novel or any work of art, we usually tend to trace the 'continuity' of theme and 'the steady progression of events in a particular direction.

The 'smaller units' that come together to make a story 'plausible' and give it a form, which will finally reach its end, are called 'archetypes' which he defines as 'a word which has been connected since Plato's time with the sense of a pattern or model used in creation.' (253) By taking refuge to the Aristotelian concept of the superiority of plot over characters where characters exist only as functions of the action,' (357) Frye tries to prove that the archetypes too by the application of 'uninhibited imagination' function as the formal grounds to build a pattern which is the end of any work of art. These patterns or arrangements, Frye says, already exist in myths and therefore, myth criticism always leads the critic to make an attempt to place the work of art in a larger universe as opposed to the naturalist criticism or impressionism where if the former tends to evaluate works as simple imitation of life, the latter limits the works to the critic's apprehensions about life and the world. While defining theme in its three different senses as 'subject,' three different senses as 'subject,' 'allegory' and 'unity,' he identifies 'plot' with 'mythos' and holds the view that we, as reader and critic, are continually involved in 'constructing a larger pattern of simultaneous significance out of what we have so far read or seen' (or experienced as the descendents of the primitive beings on earth).

This innate tendency to relate the text in hand to the universal text (myth) is as natural in the reader-critic as it is present in the writer-creator when he is creating the text, though often at the unconscious level. It is proved by the fact that imagination, 'the power that produces art,' (355) does never produce a work of 'random fantasy' but the outcome is always a 'highly conventionalized art' in a specific structure full of sense of judgement and precision. This happens because the writer has to make the stories 'sufficiently plausible or credible to a sophisticated audience.' (356) The beginning announces the end and then everything is subordinated to achieve that end. This structure is again a borrowing from myths, though it must always be kept in mind that myth, as 'a form of verbal art' (360) or 'the matrix of literature' (363) or the artistic presentation of 'nature in a humanized form,' (361) does never long for 'plausible' or 'logical' progression because it tells the stories of 'gods or other beings larger in power than humanity.' (360) So it is not like the life on earth, rather it presents a world which the writer wants the human world to be like. Myth, therefore, is the provider of 'the main outlines and the circumference of a verbal universe,' (362) which is used as the chief source and is ultimately exploited by literature.

While defining the concept of 'displacement' Frye suggests that there are certain works of art which directly show their allegiance to myth, whereas others do not explicitly suggest their borrowing from any particular myth to appear more credible, logically motivated or normally acceptable—life like' (365) but these realistic works are more conscious of a mythical pattern because life presents 'a continuum' and does never suggest a plausible conclusion. The myth critics, therefore, by interpreting the works of art in mythical and archetypal terms try to work out certain patterns that speak for the fundamental natural psychology and basic cultural values that are contained in the oldest rituals and traditions which began with the beginning of life on earth and still continue to exist. Just as language is a pattern of symbols, myths are also a symbolic codification of the most primitive universal aspirations and feelings that emanate from the human situation on earth. Unlike the New Critics who concentrate upon the texture and symmetry of a text, the myth critics go back to the prehistoric period in search of a connection that integrates the work of art by making it a part of the whole.

The text that I have chosen to discuss is Girish Karnad's play *The Fire and the Rain.*[2] It is an avowed representation of 'the myth of Yavakri (or Yavakrita)' that occurs in chapters 135-138 of the *Vana Parva* (Forest Canto) of the *Mahabharata*. It is a very short story narrated by the ascetic Lomasha to the Pandavas when they are living in exile. After churning the myth for thirty-seven years in mind, Girish Karnad decided to develop a play on this myth when he was commissioned by the Gutherie Theatre, Minneapolis, U.S.A.

The last line of Act Two 'the rites begin again. The stage darkens' (38) speaks for the archetypal pattern that gives life a coherent structure on earth and makes it a continuous phenomenon. It is further elaborated and substantiated by Nittilai's statement in Act Three when we are left with no option to answer her final question but a negative one as 'Perhaps nowhere, never' for she says:

> Yavakri avenges his father's shame by attacking your (Arvasu's) sister-in-law. Your father avenges her by killing Yavakri. Your brother kills your father. And now you in your turn want vengeance—where will it all end? (43)

The play begins with the 'Prologue' where the priests are involved in offering oblations to the fire as the seven-year long fire sacrifice is on to please the god of rains, Indra and to save the drought-hit land from further catastrophes. Paravasu, a young man of twenty-eight, is the Chief Priest who is conducting and guiding the ritual with full dedication. The priests are singing the hymns and are creating a more pious atmosphere. When the afternoon session ends and the priests are returning to take a rest for a while, a courtier appears followed by the Actor-Manager, who is the head of a touring drama troupe. The troupe is waiting outside the city gates when the Actor-Manager has come to seek permission from the King to stage a play in honour of the fire sacrifice.' But the King becomes angry when the Actor-Manager tells that Arvasu, Pravasu's brother will also participate as an actor because Paravasu had already forbidden his entrance in the premises of the sacrifice. But as the Priests are insisting for the performance, King refers it to Paravasu for his decision. Actor-Manager conveys the message of Arvasu to Paravasu that though he is a Brahmin by birth after killing his father, 'a noble Brahmin,' he 'stands tarnished' and therefore be allowed to act in the play. King grows suspicious for 'As a sacrifice approaches completion, demons gather in the shadows' (4) and therefore, 'to permit a condemned criminal in the vicinity of sacrificial fires, to risk at this stage' (4) but Paravasu consents for the performance by saying that 'Perhaps the sacrifice needs danger.' (4) The performance begins and among the audience are the King, Paravasu, the priests and the general public behind them. Arvasu, a young man of eighteen calls Nittilai, a hunter girl of fourteen and says that 'this is fiction borrowed from the myths' (4) which they are going to present but the 'real play began somewhere else' (4) about a month ago when he was planning to meet the elders of Nittilai's tribe to persuade them for their marriage. The Prologue ends with the appearance of Nittilai on the stage.

Act One opens with Nittilai training Arvasu to face the elders courageously. Arvasu is depressed thinking as to how he will utter these words like 'I want to take her [Nittilai] as my wife. I am potent. I can satisfy all her needs' (5) and that too 'in plain, loud words' (5) before 'a smirking, nudging, surging multitude' (5) because he is a Brahmin and not a young man of the tribe. He suspects if the young men of the tribe become violent and chase him away but Nittilai encourages him by telling that her father likes him and has already warned 'the young men not to get carried away.' (5) Nittilai plays sensible for when Arvasu pulls her nearer, she reminds him that they are not yet married and therefore should try to maintain a proper distance. When they reach near the hermitage of Yavakri, a blind man, called Andhaka, a Sudra gatekeeper, is sitting by the gate. Arvasu tries to feign his identity by moving in a zigzag motion but Andhaka with able ears recognizes him by his movements and congratulates them for their decision to marry each other against all odds and above all barriers of caste and creed.

Arvasu tells about how he decided to marry Nittilai for when he discovered that he was not so bright as his father Raibhya, uncle, brother Paravasu or cousin Yavakri were and that he liked dancing, singing and acting and being with Nittilai forever, he resolved to marry her and live life according to his own wishes. At the same time, no one cares for him in the family except his brother whom he owes everything that he has. Then there is a good deal of discussion about Yavakri's ten-year-long ascetic practices which he has done while living away from the world. Now he has gained certain powers by pleasing Lord Indra and has gone beyond his predecessors in knowledge, as Andhaka claims. Nittilai checks Andhaka by arguing 'why are Brahmins so secretive about everything' that 'their fire sacrifices are conducted in covered enclosures' (10) and also that if 'Lord Indra appeared to Yavakri and Indra is their God of Rain, why didn't Yavakri ask for a couple of good showers' (10) to revive this parched land? Her questions remain unanswered till the end. When they are about to leave, Andhaka tells Arvasu that Yavakri had asked him to meet him when the sun is 'exactly' overhead, 'Neither earlier. Nor later.' (11)

The place of action shifts to 'another part of the stage, representing the hermitage of Raibhya, father of Arvasu.' (12) Vishakha, about twenty-six years old wife of Paravasu, is seen 'filling water in a metal urn.' (12) She 'must nave been an attractive woman once, but now looks angry and haggard.' When she is about to move, Yavakri comes in her way. She avoids him and asks him to let her go but Yavakri requests her to have a dialogue with him. When she reminds him that she is married now and cannot talk to 'a stranger' like that, Yavakri says that it was 'the first piece of news' (12) that he heard and was shattered. Vishakha unwillingly stays for a moment to say that he has now become a great ascetic for he is gifted with the 'Universal Knowledge.' Yavkari mocks at such high-sounding phrases and bursts vehemently against all these affairs of pretension and hypocrisy:

> Universal knowledge! What a phrase! It makes me laugh now. . . . You go into the jungle. . . . You stand in a circle of fire. The pressure of your austerities forces the god to grant you your wish. And you get universal knowledge. Victory! (Pause) It wasn't at all like that, you know. (13)

He describes the hell-like life that one has to live in the jungle with no one as companion but flies, ants, leeches and vipers. He has returned after mastering 'a few secret arts' and with a firm realization that knowledge can be acquired through experience and never through penance, he concludes his statement by recounting the moment when he had gone to her house to bid her adieu before leaving for the jungle and how she had poured her love on him and that how he still longs for that moment which is still lurking on his consciousness as an intoxicated Vishakha laughs at his teenage fantasies but she realizes that both of them are 'hungry for words' and want to talk open-heartedly like a lover and a beloved:

> I live in this hermitage, parched and wordless, like a she-devil. And words are like water—precious. I was afraid to bathe. Now I want to drown. (15)

She narrates the story of her marriage with Paravasu and the bliss that he gave her for a year but from the very first day of the second year he became silent and was engrossed in his 'search' and used her body and his own as the experiment ground, 'as instruments in a search.' (16) Finally he left as the Chief Priest of the fire sacrifice and never returned in these seven years. She has simply turned into a lifeless breathing being, 'dry like cinder.' (16) She hands herself over to Yavakri as she is 'ready to burst into flames at a breath.' (16) They recede 'behind a dry champak tree on the bank' when Nittilai and Arvasu enter.

Arvasu is keen to meet Yavakri before leaving for Nittilai's village to meet her elders. The sun is exactly overhead and they are waiting for Yavakri for he has promised to meet him when Nittilai points to Vishakha's pot. Arvasu is astonished to see it there. Nittilai discovers the footprints going towards the champak tree and enquires if Arvasu's brother, Paravasu, is back. When Arvasu responds in negative, she senses the situation and asks him to leave. But Arvasu goes behind the tree and returns with a wry face followed by Vishakha in torn clothes and back 'covered with mud.' (18) She leaves the place immediately without looking at anybody. When Nittilai looks angrily at Yavakri, he forecasts that she will be 'dead within the month' (18) and exits.

When Vishakha reaches the hermitage followed by Arvasu, her father-in-law, Raibhya had already returned and has been waiting for her. He is shocked to see her in such a condition and starts kicking her while interrogating about who else other than Arvasu and Nittilai was present there. When Vishakha calmly accepts the presence of Yavakri, Raibhya takes it as a challenge from Yavakri and, therefore, invokes the 'Kritya' and sends a Brahma Rakshasa to kill him. Yavakri can be saved only by hiding himself in his father's hermitage for twenty-four hours and if he manages to escape death, Raibhya 'shall accept defeat and enter fire.' (20) Vishakha runs to save him when he is involved in meditation. When she tells him the entire story, he is happy that his uncle had to use all his powers to kill him and is confident that with the help of his 'consecrated' water, he will be able to make Brahma Rakshasa 'numb' and 'powerless.' He is full of hatred against Raibhya's family as he tells Vishakha that his father, not Raibhya, was one of the most learned men in the land,' (22) 'the most brilliant mind' (22) but this unscrupulous brother, Raibhya 'grabbed all the honours' (22) which his father really deserved. Even the Chief Priestship of the fire sacrifice should have been offered to his father but 'that too went to Paravasu.' (22) Vishakha, like a true beloved, tries to pacify his feelings by saying that 'the past is gone' (22) but he asserts:

> The past isn't gone. It is here inside me. The time has come to show the world what my father's son is capable of. This is my moment. (23)

And then defines his concept of knowledge in unequivocal terms:

> This obsession. This hatred. This venom. All this is me. I'll not deny anything of myself. I want knowledge so I can be vicious, destructive! (23)

Vishakha is shocked when he confesses that the events are all fabricated by him and nothing 'happened accidentally,' (23) that he called Arvasu 'at the river-bank at the right moment' (23) and her father-in-law back and also that had she not yielded to him willingly, he would have had to take 'her by force.' (23) So Raibhya interpreted his action correctly that this was an outright challenge to his family. Vishakha is overawed by this gesture of Yavakri. When he is 'pacing restlessly' and waiting for the Brahma Rakshasa to arrive, she quietly picks up his Kamandalu and pours the entire 'sanctified' water down and leaves him wailing like a helpless beast. When he starts running towards his father's hermitage, the Brahma Rakshasa arrives and spears him.

Act two opens with 'Nittilai's brother and a couple of his friends' (26) waiting for Arvasu in the village square. The council of Elders had already dispersed after waiting for the whole day and Nittilai's marriage was finally fixed up with a youngman of her tribe. Arvasu prays the brother to let him meet Nittilai and the elders to explain his situation but all in vain. Brother asks him to leave the village at the earliest. Arvasu returns to his hermitage. In the same night, when Raibhya is still awake, Paravasu enters the hermitage covered in a black rug carrying a bow and quiver of arrows on his back. Raibhya is taken aback at his appearance for still a month is left for the fire sacrifice to end. He scolds Paravasu for his 'usual insolence' (29) and 'wilful transgression of the rules.' (29) When Raibhya and Arvasu leave the place for Paravasu and Vishakha to be alone, Vishakha candidly accepts what she had done. Paravasu does not react to it the way a husband will normally do. When she asks him as to why she went away like that, he explains:

> The formal sacrifice is a formal rite. Structured. It involves no emotional acrobatics from the participants. The process itself will bring Indra to me. (31)

Vishakha tells him that she is 'sick of silence' (32) and therefore, wants to live among the human beings, like human beings, not among semi-gods who are always silent and don't feel and think like a human being. She further tells Paravasu that when he was invited as the Chief Priest of the fire sacrifice, Raibhya felt humiliated and that there is no one to bear his lustful vengeance but Vishakha herself. She, therefore, urges Paravasu to kill her to complete the rites with 'human sacrifice.' But Paravasu, instead of killing her, kills his own father Raibhya because he believes that Raibhya killed Yavakri because he wanted to disturb him in the last stages of the sacrifice. Paravasu calls Arvasu who is standing near the tamarind hill and cursing himself for the delay due to the bath that he had to take after cremating Yavakri, for being a Brahmin, he could not meet Nittilai and her elders in that 'unclean' condition. Paravasu lies to him that he has killed his father mistaking him for 'a wild animal' and orders Arvasu to perform the penitential rites because he will have to return because 'the sacrifice must go.' (35) Vishakha warns Arvasu not to accept his orders but Arvasu accepts. While returning to the sacrificial site, Brahma Rakshasa meets him and demands his release because he is created by his father and since he has killed him, it is his duty to complete what is left by his father. Paravasu mocks at him and enters the sacrificial enclosures where no unnatural spirits can enter. When Arvasu returns home after completing the funeral rites and does not find Vishakha in the hermitage, he goes to meet Paravasu. Paravasu maltreats him and when he, like simple and innocent brother, says that his father was killed 'at the hands of his son,' he starts shouting:

> Patricide—patricide! What is he doing in these sanctified precincts? Throw him out—Out! Out! Demon! (38)

Before Arvasu could explain anything to the crowd, he was thrown out.

Act Three opens in the outskirts of the city, where sick Arvasu is lying on the ground with other 'starving villagers.' (40) Nittilai, who left her husband's house after listening to the 'terrible stories' about Arvasu, had been nursing him for the last three days with the help of the Actor-Manager's family. Arvasu realizes: "I worshipped my brother. And he betrayed me. I let you down and you risk everything for my sake." (41)

He wants to meet Paravasu once again and extract the reason for the way he behaved with him. He thinks that everything hap·pened like a well-planned conspiracy against him because he wanted to marry Nittilai and everyone was against it:

> So, first a corpse curls itself round my ankles. Yavakri. Then it's Father. Bodies drenched in blood. Like rats that pour out during the plague and die vomiting blood. . . . Can't you see the design in it all? Corpses pursuing me—evil, like a stink emanating from that sacrifice. (43)

He wants to stop Paravasu from acting as the Chief Priest because he has made him 'an unregenerate sinner in the eyes of the world, a killer,' (44) whereas the reality was that Paravasu was the killer of his father and a staunch hypocrite. Nittilai calms him down and makes fuss of the revenge motive that has become a permanent feature of his family. Actor-Manager comes to enquire about Arvasu's health and Nittilai leaves to make arrangements for the journey. Arvasu convinces the Actor-Manager that he can act well by showing his dance. Nittilai 'comes rushing in, frightened' (48) for she has seen her brother and husband who must have come to the city in search of her. So she decides to hide herself in the jungle when Arvasu will be visible preparing for the play 'The Triumph of Lord Indra.' This is the play for which the Actor-Manager has gone to seek permission from the King in the Prologue. The play is about how Lord Indra, the King of Gods betrayed his brother, Vishwarupa, the King of Men after inviting him as a guest in a fire sacrifice organized in honour of Brahma, their father and how Vritra, the third son of Brahma and the King of Nether World reacted to it.

When the Epilogue begins, we find Arvasu as Vritra, Actor-Manager as Indra and his limping brother as Vishwarupa. When Indra pierces his thunderbolt through Vishwarupa's back on the stage, Paravasu cannot restrain himself and reacts like a mad person when Brahma Rakshasa appears beside him. Then the mask of Vritra grips Arvasu's consciousness and he resolves to destroy the whole affair and Indra. In the meantime, Paravasu, watching this stampede as 'people start rushing into the burning pavilion' and 'are eating and drinking the food kept for the gods,' 'calmly walks into the blazing enclosure.' (57) Nittilai comes and taking off Vritra's mask from Arvasu's face, controls him. Her husband along with her brother steps out of the crowd and 'slashes her throat in one swift motion.' (58) Suddenly the voice of Indra is heard from the skies. He is impressed by the way Arvasu 'challenged Indra and then pursued him . . . in the play' (59) and is ready to grant a boon to him. Arvasu gets confused for he wants Nittilai back, people demand rain and Brahma Rakshasa prays for his final release from the bondage of birth and death. Arvasu ultimately requests for the release of Brahma Rakshasa for he believes that Nittilai too must have gone for it. So 'the wheel of Time' rolls forward and the play ends when it starts raining.

The play, consisting of three acts beginning with the Prologue and concluding with the Epilogue, establishes certain archetypal patterns. This is certain that the play is based on a myth and it involves different images and motifs that make it functional. The water imagery is the most central to the theme of the play for it describes the drought-hit area, which is symbolically not qualified for fertility and growth. It is the rain for which the whole affair is organized. The image of sun when it is 'exactly' overhead is very significantly used for it not only just precedes the climax but also is used as the moment which Yavakri chooses to attack upon the honour of the family of Raibhya. Two images of archetypal woman are presented in the play in the characters of Nittilai and Vishakha where the former represents the positive aspects of the Mother Earth full of warmth, protection and nourishment and the latter though full of positive quailties, is soon transformed into the archetypal terrible mother full of positive sensuousness, sexual urge, fear and destruction. She instigates her husband to kill his father. The archetypal wise old man is presented in the character of Andhaka, who is wise as well as patient. Yavakri represents the archetypal shadow figure of trickster or a fraud. He turns the story in unexpected direction and creates confusion and disorder. He is full of venom and hatred and does not hesitate to manipulate the emotions of Vishakha, then an innocent beloved. His challenge is so brutal which only a hard-core criminal can think of.

The protagonist of the play, Arvasu is the most archetypal of all. He suffers for others and pays for what he had never committed. He is the saviour of the parched land, bringer of rain, fertility and a life purer than what it was till now. So he has to undergo a series of ordeals to clean the dirt and clear the confusion. He does everything: he cremates the dead body of Yavakri, he performs the obsequies of his own father, though it should have been done by Paravasu, saves the sanctity of fire sacrifice by setting it on fire because if completed by Paravasu, the murderer of Yavakri, it would have rained 'blood' and finally releases the Brahma Rakshasa. So Arvasu is the real archetypal sacrificial scapegoat who sacrifices everything that is his own including Nittilai for the sins, pretensions and hypocrisies of others and brings rain and happiness back to the country.

NOTES

1. B. Das and J.M. Mohanty, *Literary Criticism: A Reading* (Calcutta: Oxford University Press, 1993), p. 368.
2. Girish Karnad, *The Fire and the Rain* (New Delhi: Oxford University Press, 1999).

Love and Betrayal in Shiv K. Kumar's *To Nun with Love and Other Stories*

SUMITA PURI
Dyal Singh (Eve.) College, University of Delhi

Indian writing in English has come a long way since the days of the 'Big Three'—Mulk Raj Anand, Raja Rao and R.K. Narayan and Indian prose fiction has made a definite mark in the new millennium. Amongst the shining glories, Shiv K. Kumar has also added lustre to the galaxy of literary stars by being a novelist, poet, playwright, short story writer, translator and critic in the same breath. Popularly known for his works *Thus Spake the Buddha*, *A River with Three Banks* and his translation, *The Best of Faiz*, Shiv K. Kumar received the prestigious Sahitya Akademi award for his collection of poetry *Trapfalls in the Sky* in 1988. In 1991, *The Journal of South Asian Literature* (Michigan) brought out a special issue on his work. In 2001 he was awarded the Padma Bhushan for his contribution to literature. The former Chairman of the Department of English at the University of Hyderabad has arrived in the literary arena this time with a collection of short stories, *To Nun with Love and Other Stories* published by Orient Longman. Most of the stories of this collection have been translated into French, Portuguese, Arabic, Urdu, Hindi, Thai and other languages.

To Nun with Love and Other Stories is a mixed bag of angst and humour. The first story "To Nun with Love" is about the platonic love of a middle-aged married man with the Nun in his daughter's school. The love experienced by the anonymous writer of the love letters to the Nun establishes the faith of man in God. In communion with the Nun, the lover comprehends man's communion with the unseen Almighty. "Point Counter Point" again contrasts platonic vs. physical love, earthly vs. divine love. Vinod is a feeble man who is easily sexually aroused, yet remains dissatisfied by his wife going the divine path. What is wickedly funny, yet true, is the fact that both the men—Vinod and the Swamy, whose disciple his wife is, are, ever ready to prowl upon her. In fact, both the stories critique the authenticity of renunciation of worldly pleasures.

Marriage as an institution becomes highly dubious and pretentious where both the members are enjoying illicit and dishonest relations elsewhere. "A Bird from Another Country," "The House of Heaven," "Hands," "Eyes," "Feet," "Hair," "Fingers," "Voices" and "Crossfire" are stories of love and betrayal. Existing marriages break due to the untrustworthiness on the part of either of the partners, mostly women.

In "A Bird from Another Country" the protagonist finds out about the infidelity of his wife many years after their marriage and the horrifying fact that his son is not actually his own, but his friend Kulbhushan's, becomes too agonizing for him to sustain and he commits suicide. In "The House of Heaven" Jim Hutchinson also feels deserted because of his wife Jane's fickleness and finds love elsewhere in Terry Patton after his traumatized wedding is over. Interestingly, a dog that he refers to as Hermes, as he is perhaps the envoy of gods, links him to Terry. The dog's faithfulness is compared to man's disloyalty when, as soon as the narrator fulfils the void in his life, the poor dog vanishes looking for another partner, just as he pursued Terry in place of his divorced wife Jane.

If the love affairs are true and genuine they end tragically with pangs of love, parting and even death of one of the lovers. In a number of stories that are titled as the various parts of the human body—"Hands," "Eyes," "Feet," "Hair," "Fingers" and so on, the author tells heart-rending and despondent tales of unhappy marriages, of men as victims of harsh and untrue wives, of women being stronger, and of men drooping erotically over other women as their carnal pleasures are ungratified with their wives. These harp upon the same tune of perfidy of both the sexes. In "Lips" it's an inter-caste affair that does not consummate in marriage and in "Eyes" it's the love of the beloved in an accident that shatters the love of Akash and Akila. In "Voices" Mr. Katyal is captivated by, and goes nuts over, voices of women. Influenced only by their 'voices' he marries and fails twice. Whether the writer tries to figure out this sense of loss in human relations through gestures of 'hands' or 'voices' or touch through 'fingers' the problem remains unsolved and he is persuaded to conclude, as he does so in "Hands" that, "It's the same pain everywhere, and I am not the only one." (87)

"The Sheikh's Bride," "The Crooked Face of Moon" and "The Ragpicker's Daughter" pick up oppressed characters—victims of Muslim laws, dowry and untouchability respectively highlighting the social crimes and their repercussions in a modern urbane set-up. The first one is about the silencing of a Muslim woman Fatima, who is married off to an old Sheikh in Dubai by her father. In the illusion that her husband is a rich man, Fatima thinks her life to be fortunate and ties the nuptial knot. Soon, she realizes that she is the third wife who is "bound to the wheel of drudgery—cooking, washing, mopping the floors." (58) She ends her life tragically, as one day the Sheikh accuses her to be a strumpet and locks her forever in the kitchen. "The Crooked Face of Moon" presents realistically the evils of the dowry system in India. Maya is the suitable bride material—beautiful and skilled in household work. Her marriage into a decent family with no demands makes her suspect the intentions of her in-laws. True to her suspicions, Maya's in-laws initiate their demands after the marriage with a room heater followed by a computer and subsequently sponsoring her husband's training in England. Her inability to free herself from the fetters that are coiling her makes her step over the iron railing of her balcony and die. In "The Ragpicker's Daughter," Shiv Kumar picks up the social injustice of untouchability by showing how the transgression of caste boundaries is still prohibited in India even though India is a secular state. When the beauty of the Ragpicker's daughter bewitches Mahesh, his parents are scandalized and naturally unwelcome the idea of their conjugal union. At once, the son is befooled with the idea that Guddi has simply disappeared with her father and Sunder, the ragpicker, is offered thirty thousand rupees to forsake the city and their lives permanently. The mockery on casteism is carried further in "The Shoe Black" where Anil Deshpande forms a bond of affinity with a shoeblack Ranga, who polishes his shoes daily. In order to extend his generosity and benevolence, he offers the shoeblack's sister Nandini the job of attendant in his bank. The author now twists the story by showing how, once again, a menial endangers the man-wife relationship and all humanitarianism goes down the drain. Comically, the Hindu custom of Rakshbandhan saves the duo from further humiliation as Nandini ties the sacred thread on the hand of the Senior Personnel Officer at the State Bank of India.

Yet the world is not so distressing and Kumar compels us to giggle at times with humorous stories like "Mrs. Williamson," "Lord Krishna" and "The Property Dealer." In contrast to 'earthly' love Mrs. Williamson is still in love with her husband who has left her for heavenly abode. Her eccentricity and whimsicality reach its heights when she wishes people to die as soon as possible so that some parting soul may convey her message of love to the soul of her dead husband. "Lord Krishna" is about an old couple that is taken care by the Deputy Director General of Police, George Samuel, in their train journey to Shimla. The policeman's act of consideration in helping them visit the temple in Chandi village on the way makes the couple resolve that he is no other than Lord Krishna reincarnate who has come to their assistance. Both of these stories compare the Hindu and Christian beliefs. The Professor of English at University of Hyderabad takes advantage of his literary background and renders a prosaic version of John Keats' *La Belle Dame Sans Merci*. Interestingly, in "The Property Dealer" Mrs. Bose acts as the seductress who mercilessly coaxes Mr. Sanjoy Das to sell his house in half the price that is previously settled. "The House" is personified as "susceptible to pain and joy" (44) as human beings are and represents one's nostalgic past that can cause pain if one clings on to it for long.

The stories take us from the Oberoi Hilton in Bombay to Chandi village near Chandigarh, from Lodi Gardens in Delhi to Oklahoma Bridge in the United States. They are also Indianized by use of Hindi words such as 'dhoti' and 'jhumka.' The shared factor in most of them remains the dynamic characterization, complex and innovative plots and the element of suspense at the end. With the use of imagery of birds, insects and animals, human frailties and follies are pointed out. The dog becomes a symbol of loyalty and faithfulness in contrast with the unfaithfulness of human beings. The drone of a bumblebee to escape becomes suggestive of the Sheikh's wife's desire to free her from the clutches of married life. Other birds, rabbits and cats denote varied human behavioural patterns. Characters are 'round' as E.M. Forster would put it and the vivid experience of the academic-turned-writer makes him employ many figures of speech—metaphors, similes and personification to paint them skilfully, ranging from Harijans to Sheikhs with fineness of detail. Men are emotional, highly romantic and impractical, desperately excited all the time. On the contrary, most of the women are highly balanced, rational, believing, "that sentiments always weakened one's will to face the harsh realities of life." (43) Like a painter, the woman's body is sketched out with great adroitness. In fact, the various body parts—hands, fingers, feet, lips, eyes and hair provide the writer a passage into the human psyche and these body parts aid him in understanding what is stored in the hidden recesses of the human mind. Social offences such as dowry, the Muslim law allowing four marriages and untouchability are also touched upon with a realistic and gloomy twist. There is silencing of the weaker sections of society—be it Maya of "The Crooked Face of Moon" or Fatima of "The Sheikh's Bride" or the ragpicker of "The Ragpicker's Daughter." The former two are suppressed and powerless to succumb to male hegemony and commit suicide and the latter is forced to forsake the city with thirty thousand rupees as a penalty for his daughter's endeavour to transgress her caste boundaries by thinking of marrying a Brahmin.

The conciseness and precision that embellish the genre of short story are prevalent in this collection. In the manner of his predecessors of the same genre—Edgar Alan Poe, Guy de Maupaussant, Anton Chekhov and his contemporary Jhumpa Lahiri, his narratives have a dramatic turn or twist at the end. Although Shiv K. Kumar is an accomplished man in real life who has enjoyed connubial bliss himself, he portrays a contrasted world of depressing love associations that end sorrowfully and even traumatically. Although they appear to be tales of the veiled secrets and sexual fancies of both the sexes, yet, concealed inside is the deep compassion and humanitarian concern of the author for human weaknesses and shortcomings and poignantly bring out the fragility and subtlety of human bonding that lead to love and betrayal. While most of them bring out a catharsis of tragic emotions, a few provide an amusing interval. If only things were not so dismal, life for each of his characters would have been better and the world a better place to live in! In all, like his previous works, *To Nun with love and Other Stories* is appealing, full of pathos and a hugely pleasurable read.

Work Cited

Shiv K. Kumar, *To Nun with Love and Other Stories* (India: Orient Longman, 2002), p.87.

Of No Fixed Certainties: Amitava Kumar's *Bombay London New York: A Literary Journey*

NEERU ANAND
Dyal Singh Eve. College, University of Delhi

"And do not call it fixity, where past and future are gathered."
T.S. Eliot "Four Quartets"

Part travelogue, part memoirs, part literary criticism, part dialogue with the self, Amitava Kumar's *Bombay London New York: A Literary Journey* (Penguin, New Delhi, 2002) is a heady concoction of multiple genres. As the title indicates, the idea of mobility is celebrated. Arrivals and departures are not so much as new beginnings and dead ends as part of a continually moving, continually changing perception of a world where fiction mingles with fact, reality becomes metaphor, imagination becomes experience, and magic realism is not so much a literary technique as a device of deifying Gandhi by the peasants of Gorakhpur way back in 1921!

Kumar jumps from one physical/ literary landscape to another at a breathless pace, examining a variety of issues—migration, displacement, liminality, marginalization, identity—in fact all the concerns of a postcolonial world. Refreshingly, his interrogation of these issues is not in an opaque jargon of some of his more celebrated colleagues but rather in a personalized idiom, his own experiences acting as a conduit. Moving backward and forward in time and space, Kumar tries to articulate the interface between the boy growing up in the backwaters of India and the man who became Professor of English in a prestigious American University.

Like other postcolonial writing, this book too has a Janus aspect. The celebration of mobility as one moves from the periphery to the centre juxtaposed with the compulsion to look back at back at one's origins in a bid to understand one's own self or history imparts a tension to the text. Further, Kumar examines the fissures in the binary oppositions of periphery / centre as the periphery for him (Patna in Bihar) is the centre for somebody like Laloo Prasad Yadav, who makes a journey from Phulwaria to Patna and thus gets "an opportunity to learn about the wider world." (55) A location can thus be both confining and liberating.

Moreover, Kumar himself, though eager to escape from the provincialism of Patna, cannot quite identify with the Anglophile cosmopolitanism of writers like Salman Rushdie or Rohinton Mistry. At the reading of this book in Florida he differentiated between "Cosmopolitan Cosmopolitan" writer and "Provincial Cosmopolitan" ones like himself. This awareness of the difference between his own origins in Patna and a Westernized Megapolis like Salman Rushdie's Bombay is crucial. One it saves Indian writing in English—whether diasporic or (for want of a better word) indigenous—from essentialisation. Secondly, it gives Kumar an opportunity to begin in his hometown of Patna.

What follows is the glimpse of an unwashed Bharat with its smells, stinks, claustrophobic customs, and lack of literary culture. This might have degenerated, obversely, into an *'exotica'* for Western readership but for the fact that Kumar not only does not glorify mothballed traditions but also salutes the spirit of the small-town people. Therefore he lauds the efforts of a writer like Pankaj Mishra who celebrates small-town India in his texts and whose inhabitants are not robbed of their dignity because of a "failure to speak proper English." (51)

Concurrently reading Mishra's *Butter Chicken in Ludhiana: Travels in small town India*, also brings into sharp focus that he is no longer the moufassil boy scared that he would be deported back home from America lest he "wrote terrible sentences" to an Indian-American who might ask for a "boddle of Bisleri wadder" to a non-plussed hotel owner. (4 and 5) This change in location accompanied by the uncertainties in concepts of home, language, culture, identity forms an integral part of his journey and the text.

Kumar extrapolates his arrival in a foreign land with that of Naipaul's and also reminiscences on a much earlier visitor—Gandhi. The juxtaposition of three arrivals at different times of history and then preserved for posterity in the words of a text gives Kumar an opportunity to discuss the life of immigrants. Drawn in the discussion are Kumar's own uncle (who migrated to America in the 60s and never returned) as also the fictional characters Mr. Biswas (modelled by Naipaul on his own father) and Jhumpa Lahiri's narrator in the story "The Third and Final Continent" (again modelled on her own father). This paralleling of literature with lived reality is central to the text. Rather pointedly, Kumar abstains from discussing canonical Anglo-American literature, but focuses on Indian writing not merely in English but also in Hindi. While stressing the multilingual nature of India, where the influences can be of/ in many languages, this also demonstrates a new assurance and self-assertiveness in Indian literature and writers. The writers discussed—ranging from Naipaul to Renu to Pankaj Mishra to Jhumpa Lahiri to Manil Suri—are all in whose works Kumar finds an echo of his own concerns. Besides a proof of Kumar's voracious appetite as regards books, this also gives him an opportunity to exorcise the bogey of writing in English which every Indian has to account for and defend. And yes, he does invoke Vikram Seth's Amit Chatterjee who so famously declared, "We are all accidents of history."

Being part of a historical movement, the first generation immigrants tried to adjust or adapt to a country where they met with contempt, ridicule and segregation. Trying to eke a living, sending pounds and dollars home to a desperate family, they felt both alienated and exiled. Kumar quotes Mira Kamdar: "India was far, far away. Airline tickets were expensive. There was no direct dial international calling, no fax machines-cum-answering machines attached to people's phones, no e-mail." (133) The lines stress a displacement and loneliness chilling to the bones. Trishanku-like, these people grasped at the only thing they felt was worth clinging to—the home they had left behind. The result was an obsessive harping on the notion of India as an ideal land and an equally obsessive clinging to rituals and rites which the home-country had paradoxically discarded. Frozen in time and eternity this delusion alternatively sustained them or shattered them like it did to Naipaul's Sardarji who cried at the appalling poverty of this area of darkness.

The subsequent generations felt more confident and sure. The western world was no longer an unfamiliar domain. Either born and brought up in a land which was no longer foreign (ironically the land their parents clung to had now become 'foreign') or new migrants, enamoured by the professionalism of the West and in easy touch with folks back home, this generation sought to chalk out an economic and physical space for themselves. (Silicon Valley is a testimony of their determination.) Giving a voice to this generation, Hanif Kureishi's *The Buddha of Suburbia* begins with, "My name is Karim Amir and I am an Englishman born and bred, almost." (121) The 'almost' at the end carries both the poignancy and confidence of a generation whose attitudes and responses are more often than not conditioned by a hyphenated wor(l)d: Indian-American, Indo-Canadian, Brown-Briton.

This hyphenated identity of people living in one land but at the same time carrying "an elsewhere" can at times lead to paranoia: of a romanticizing of one's "elsewhere"—culture/ home (and by an extension the Nation State) as pure and pristine, a veritable Garden of Eden before outside influences hissed in the ear. Warning of such "soft nostalgia" being transformed into "hard fundamentalism," which in extreme cases can result in tragedies like that of September 11, Kumar takes pains to expose the underbelly of the (supposedly) noble Indian culture—sexual harassment, repressed sexuality, dowry deaths, and honour killings; is contemptuous of Bollywood films glorifying an Innocent India (that does not exist anywhere but in the imagination) vis-a-vis a viciously decadent Western world from which the unsuspecting Indian better return. Literary texts deny this easy (and essentially false) polarization, and unlike movies focus on adaptation and amalgamation. This broadening of sensibility is valorized and the dismantling of "Sinful West/Virtuous East" appreciated.

However, if Kumar is wary of the soft-pedalling of nostalgia, he is also not enamoured by the rhetoric of globalization. He critiques the idea of the "benefits of globalization." Is it merely the opening of call-centres which provide job opportunities, but also impose upon the people an alternate identity and lifestyle (change of name, fake accents, erratic work hours) that can lead to schizophrenia and maladjustment? Or is it the Dish which has penetrated even the rural hinterland with its intellectually vacuous Western T.V. shows? Or is it the creation of Desire? While the Western world benefits by the creation of new markets, for the many people living in poverty-stricken areas of the world it presents a false picture of America/ England as the proverbial El Dorado which they have to reach at any cost.

But unlike the remote button, the First World does not provide easy access to everybody. Depending on its wants, it can import unskilled labour (slave trade, indentured labour) at one time or skilled professionals at another. The rest it rejects. And thus many faceless, nameless young men end up like Mohammed Ayaz, who tried to smuggle into England by hiding in the chambers above the wheels of a Boeing, but ended up as a corpse in a car park. As Ayaz's father remarked, "They don't give visas to poor like us." (187)

But those who are given visas and yet decide to return, are they all to be termed failures? And those who do not return, are they forgetful of their duties? One detects a note of sorrow and perhaps of guilt through Kumar's narrative. The neglect of his parents and thousands like them who live in the hope of seeing their children return and whose life can be measured by the rings of the telephone. Thus, in the vehement assertion of the son that he would return to India, in Satyajit Ray's "Aparajit," Kumar finds his own experience, knowing that the words are hollow, carrying within them the impossibility of returning to a space that one has outgrown. There are no easy answers and Kumar has no certainty about any of the responses of "Going Away" or "Coming Home." He leaves it in that enigmatic sentence (significantly not his own utterance but that of a neighbour), "I am very happy that I came to this country. I am very happy that I am going back." (206)

Gordimer's *The Late Bourgeois World*: Revolutionary Veneer over Conventional Gender Roles

RASHMI GAUR
Indian Institute of Technology, Roorkee

Gordimer had started writing at an early age. Having identified herself with the values and patterns of life propagated by the British literature at the early stage, she soon realized that instead of imitating the British writers, she should write about her "own life," which may seem common place to her, but is "extremely exotic" to the outside world.[1] She takes up themes based on the everyday life of the South African people—black as well as white—who, crippled by the burdens of colour and class discrimination, have to struggle within and against an oppressive capitalist system, which still propagates and preserves feudal norms of socio-political structures. Gordimer has sensitively painted the South African sensibility as an insider, which makes her descriptions authentically and critically realistic. In her later works she has vociferously talked about the strong emergent feelings of national identity that pervade the South African society despite its very apparent social, economic and racial divisions.[2] Any novel based on such themes would essentially be an expression of protest, "The theme of racial conflict can, all too easily, become an obsessive one, the humiliation and revenges of oppression can drown everything else like sex in pornography, closing all characters and compassion in the whirlpool."[3] Gordimer, however, does not lose the objectivity of her vision. *The Late Bourgeois World* presents the turbulent individual and social psyche of a society, in which the black and white segments are constantly being churned in a cesspool of uncontrollable events; it also represents her anger against apartheid, as well as her worries for the growth of developing national identity.

II

The temptation to limit oneself to an anti-apartheid reading of Nadine Gordimer's fiction is overwhelming, as she records a country's painful transition from an oppressive racist autocracy to a problem-ridden infant democracy—but to do so will be constricting and superficial. In her Nobel Lecture "Writing and Being," delivered on December 7, 1991, she has quoted Nikos Kazantzakis, "Art is the representation, not of the body but of the forces which created the body."[4] She has further remarked that a writer has to be understood in relation to the nature of perceivable reality and "what is beyond—imperceivable reality."[5] She often reveals situations in which "reality takes another course and we are caught in our roles and expectations, in the traps of skin colour, class, family, and the body itself."[6] She sensitively and sympathetically paints those who try to escape these traps—Liz Van Den Sandt, the protagonist of *The Late Bourgeois World* is a divorcee mother who suddenly becomes an underground agent. She represents a voice that, to quote Joya Uraizee, "perpetually resists within a discourse that is evolving and shifting."[7] She constantly reconstructs the past, evaluating it with different and shifting focuses, to recreate her present, both personal and collective, seeking all the time, some elusive completion/ fulfilment. The narrative is not quite straightforward, though its perspective is not skewed either. It puts forth the story of Liz, a divorcee whose ex-husband drowns himself in the sea. Our major impressions about Liz are formed by her descriptions of Max and their life together. Liz is in the background and one has to interpret her life by concentrating on the absence of any direct narrative about her own self. It is not till she is contacted by Luke, an activist of the black-nationalist movement, that he tries to coherently put together her choices about life—even then her autonomous self-hood does not come to the foreground. Her affinity with the cause which was dear to her ex-husband is exhibited categorically, but it has been constantly overshadowed by her subconscious acceptance of her own gender inferiority.

In the early pages of *The Late Bourgeois World*, Gordimer's investigation of a manacled existence and the ultimate futility of protest suggests the nightmarish vision of a constricting society. The early descriptions of the novel also contain some traces of Orwellian scepticism. Max's rich, influential background makes the contrast more apparent. His father, Theo van Den Sandt, represents the traditional white elite of the South African society. He is a rich businessman and a successful politician, taking it for granted that his son shall obviously carry forward the tradition of white supremacy and racial exploitation. When he calls for a united South Africa going forward to an era of progress and prosperity for all, he means the welfare of the English speaking white people and "higher wages and bigger cars for them." (26) Max's mother conveys the same inferences when she speaks of 'We South Africans.' Gordimer has obviously portrayed a society in which the slavery of the many pays for the liberty and luxury of a few. Max protests against the repressive value code handed out to him by his background. Non-agentic protest gestures of superficial intellectual empathy are meaningless for him. When he proposes toast to his sister Queenie and her bridegroom, he talks openly about moral sclerosis (32). He participates in protests, gets arrested, released and then finally arrested again for having made a bomb. For his parents he is dead from this point—his arrest on a charge of sabotage is a public shame they can not live with. Their notions of social prestige have entrapped them, "the Van Den Sandts interpret honour as something that exists in the eyes of others; you can do each other to death, in private; shame or pain came only from what leaks out." (28) Max takes the dirt done in the name of this sanctity upon himself, "tarred and feathered himself with it." (25) His ultimate break down under torture becomes a prelude to his suicide, underlining the futility as well as the significance of the only available option of preserving the residues of his tattered self respect and incoherent indignation against the system. The novel may not have the transcending serenity of Leo Tolstoy's Resurrection, or the pragmatic optimism of Alexander Solzhenitsyn's "We Will Never Die," but it does contain a definitive positive surge, a determination to continue the fight. As a novel of protest *The Late Bourgeois World* is a beautiful novel. The note of protest registers a demand of political equality only—strangely and ironically it is silent about the conceptual and/or actual need of gender equality, without which no society can be considered to be truly liberated.

A feminist reading of the novel evinces that within the given calculus of individual and society as portrayed by Gordimer it is nearly impossible for a woman to free herself from the stereotypes of conventionally promoted gender roles. The novel portrays how the structural features of the social milieu ensure that women are fitted into pre-defined roles and are conditioned to live through the essence of what is traditionally defined as womanhood. The present paper studies Gordimer's *The Late Bourgeois World* from this perspective.

III

The coercive force of assumptions culturally accepted by a society restricts an autonomous understanding of the self by a woman. Commercial publishing strategies often sell women's writings as subversive, sexual autobiographies—the autobiographies of gender.[8] But even when women authors present active, thinking, speaking women characters, their writings are sometimes inhibited by the conventional indoctrination of treating themselves as secondary or inferior beings, seeking validation/ justification of their desires/actions by gaining male approval. Society has traditionally fostered self-effacement in women. Even highly accomplished and talented women often find it hard to combat this subtle social conditioning. The deep rooted indoctrination of a patriarchal society corrupts the objectivity of women's psyche too; affecting the complexity of her relations with her past, present and even future experiences, controlling the pace of her relationships, transitions and even climaxes of her personal life. Throughout one's reading of *The Late Bourgeois World*, the reader gets the impression that despite possessing an intellectual bent of mind Liz is unable, also at times unwilling, to free herself from conventional gendered limitations in more ways than one. The tradition of self-effacement often creates doubts, as we know through Liz's stream of consciousness:

> Even though I know I'm a dammed intelligent woman—by far the most intelligent female he's ever had any sort of dealings with—and that a relationship with a woman of my kind implies the acceptance not only of intellectual equality but also coeval commonsense (none of the patronizing affection toward precocious feminine cleverness)—in spite of this, even when I'm holding up my end in discussion a shade better than he is, there's a sort of backward glance, in me, at my performance before him. (67)

This self-doubt—obtaining justification of one's desire by male counterparts, getting their decisions whetted by male approval—is an inescapable part of the conditioned feminine psyche, examples of which are visible in Liz's reactions to various emotions and situations demanding decision. There are sufficient textual clues to indicate that Liz had imbibed conventional feminine psyche in her formative years. Binary opposition of male and female worlds, and the superiority of the male world is quite evident in her cognitive patterns. She recalls, "At eighteen I was quite sure, of course. I would be married and have a baby." (36) Marriage is the ultimate panacea for her:

> Max might not have been the man according to specifications, but the situation, deep in my subconscious, matched the pattern I'd been given to go by. The concept of marriage as shelter remained with me, even if it were only to be shelter from parents and their ways. There, whatever the walls were made of, I should live a woman's life, which was?—a life lived among women like my mother, attached to a man like my father. (36)

Marriage is the "destiny traditionally offered to women by society"[9] and the gender dimensions of this belief act disastrously for women. Liz has been brought up to live among women, "as middle class women with their shopping and social and household concerns comfortably do," (36) but her circumstances have forced her to lead an independent life she is not equipped to face.

Her background has emphatically nurtured her to be a woman, not to be an individual. When the situation demands a direct decision, she suddenly feels diffident and defensive. At crucial moments her actions are governed by her gendered psyche, instead of being governed by the rational calculations of clandestine revolutionary goals. By the time Liz realizes that most of what she has learnt from her family and background, has "turned out to be hopelessly obsolete" (36), it is rather late.

IV

Literature reflects human consciousness and portrays the pervasive culture of the land, though it may be an indirect rendition. Susan Sontag has rightly commented that even in modern times, "when most artists and critics have discarded the theory of art as representation of an outer reality in favour of the theory of art as subjective expression, the main feature of the mimetic theory persists."[10] Within Gordimer's narrative, the descriptions of routine life often function as markers—of what is there and what isn't. In the "what is there" category we witness the practice of such social norms as are accepted as habits, and are never questioned for being discriminatory against women. The "what isn't there" category also has a discernible presence beneath the narrative superstructure of the text which a sensitive reader can clearly identify. Ruth Parkin-Gounelas comments:

> Fiction, of course, has always been attentive to the possibility of imagining "what isn't there," as fantasy writing has continued to demonstrate throughout the centuries. Within a context of the postmodern challenge to a metaphysics of presence, this attraction has clearly received new impetus, with the result that presence in physical / spatial terms, as well as in terms of the temporal category of "the present," has increasingly been depicted as vulnerable to forms of haunting. Other places and other times, the future as well as the past, have a tendency to creep in and take over, giving a sense of what has been described recently as spectrality.[11]

Spectrality is a term used by Jacques Derrida in his *Specters of Marx* (1993), and has for the past decade come to indicate concepts of haunting that disturb categories such as past-present, absence-presence, anteriority-origin.[12] The haunting domination of the traditional gender based roles, particularly in the context of Liz's characterization, becomes apparent in a gendered reading of *The Late Bourgeois World*. In this novel one finds traces of biological essentialism, as well as of the social role theory, which holds that men and women become masculine or feminine through social conditioning, and learn the gender role that relates to one's biological sex through one's "interaction with social structures, such as the family, schools, the media and so on."[13] Inside the kaleidoscopically shifting images of one's own self, the unconscious and the conscious are embedded together within the contingencies of history and place.

Gordimer's novel is a sensitive commentary on the feminine psyche and its expectations. Liz was seventeen when she had met Max. Her father owned a small shop. Her parents were gratified to have her 'marry into' the Van Den Sandts, even though she had "spoiled the dignity of the alliance somewhat by being pregnant before the wedding." (60) The son of a wealthy M.P. was a son-in-law, most of the small town people were envious of. Liz herself does not expect anything beyond a pure materialistic interpretation of what she terms as "truth and beauty" in her relationship with Max:

> but I knew there must be things more worth having than these, and an object in life less shameful than palming them off on people who knew nothing better to desire. The shoddy was my sickening secret. And then I found that Max knew all about it, that the house he lived in, and what went on there, his surroundings, though richer and less obviously unattractive, were part of it, too, and that this quality of life was apparently what our fathers and grandfathers had fought two wars abroad and killed black men in 'native' wars of conquest here at home, to secure from us. Truth and beauty—good God, that's what I thought he would find, that's what I expected of Max. (61)

In a gendered society, marriage means different things for men and women. A woman is expected to ensure "the even rhythm of the days and the continuity of the home."[14] Her emotional subordination is taken for granted. Liz accepts her secondary role without questioning—while Spears, William Xaba and Max sit around "all day Sunday under the apricot tree" (70) discussing the modalities and maneuvers of the revolution, she silently cooks for them all. Liz is sometimes confused, owing to the contradiction between societal expectations/definitions and her own gut feelings, and comments on it, "I don't know whether Max loved me. He wanted to make love with me, of course. And he wanted to please me—and, he wanted my approval, my admiration for whatever he did. . . . This business of living for each other, that one hears about, it can just as well be living for the sight of one's self in the other's eyes. . . . 'Love' was the name I was given for it, but I don't know that it always fits my experience." (49) She resents Max's relationships with different women, but is too diffident to challenge them. His intimate relationships with Eve king, Roberta Weininger and Felicity cause her pain and to balance it she has one or two affairs of her own, "I suppose I thought of redressing the balance—some such expedient. But this again was the use of measures designed for a situation that had very little bearing on the realities of ours." (53) Max, on the other hand, views these relationships from the perspective of an egotist male. Liz tries to rationalize Max's flirtations, but finds herself unable to totally suppress her resentment:

> there was only one reason why Max made love to her. He knew it and I knew it. He needed approval and admiration so much that he was prepared to throw in a good fuck as payment. . . . I used to think of it when we were making love. And I couldn't give the approval and admiration. (52)

V

Another facet of traditional patriarchal norms is that the young child is always considered to be the sole responsibility of the mother. Its rearing process is never linked with a father's routine tasks. A crying/sick/helpless child is an irritant for the father, whereas the mother is expected to shoulder all such tasks willingly. Gordimer has also realistically portrayed this aspect of male conditioning. In order to support the family, Liz has to work for longer hours; leaving Bobo, their son, in Max's care.

Max is careless in his handling of the child, "he'd go on to some yard or house and dump Bobo with a set of faces or a pair of arms—anybody's—the baby had never seen before . . . left Bobo as he used to drop a bicycle or toy for the servants to pick up from the Van Den Sandt's lawn." (43) Bobo becomes an unwanted presence when Max tries to systematically "get down" what Spears talks about African socialism. Liz has recorded her reaction with a sense of helplessness:

> Max and Spears talked late into the nights and everyday Max wrote and recast from notes and memory. That was the time I came home from work and found Max yelling back at screaming Bobo. He had been trying to work all afternoon against the baby's noisy games and interruptions. Max's face was a child's mask of hysterical frustration. I took Bobo and walked in the streets with him, but there was nothing I could do for the face of Max. (48)

When on being told of Max's death Bobo suddenly blurts out, "I feel sorry I didn't love him," it can be taken as a normal and spontaneous reaction of the child whose father could never provide the much needed affection and supportive companionship.

VI

Liz's separation from Max should also be understood within its cultural milieu, and not necessarily as a sign of mental independence. In fact, Liz's constant dependence on men for emotional fulfilment clearly signifies her inability to transcend the gender stereotypes. Subversiveness of women is a position, which can also be used as a tool for analyzing the extent and hold of patriarchal dictates on women's psyche in diversified spheres. Liz relies on Graham after her separation from Max—not only for physical gratification, but also for proper shaping up her life, "If I wanted a man, here, at this time, in this country, could I find a better one?" (37) Alone, she feels inadequate. Her association with men, rather dependence on and longing for men, makes her feel an inner completion. When Luke and Reba try to seek her help, she readies herself for it after some deliberation. Her zealous desire to help the African liberation is tinged equally with her inner desire to be accepted as a woman first. In her dialogue with Luke, the sexual innuendoes are always implicit. Liz is always conscious of the sexual undertone to Luke's wheedling, cajoling, challenging confrontation (86). She enjoys Luke's admiring, kidding gaze (77). Like other white South African women who get to know black men, she feels titillated and yet safe (82). Luke's flirting game is a welcome break for her from her daily routine. Even while she decides to use her power of attorney over her grandmother's account to launder the sympathizer's money from abroad, her hankering for some closeness is quite palpable:

> A sympathetic white woman hasn't got anything to offer him—except the footing she keeps in the good old white reserve of banks and privileges. And a return he comes with the smell of the smoke of braziers in his clothes. Oh yes, and it's quite possible he'll make love to me, next time or some time. That's part of the bargain. It's honest, too, like his vanity, his lies, the loans he doesn't pay back: it's all he's got to offer me. It would be better if I accepted gratefully. . . . Perhaps it would be better than what I've had—or got. Suits me better, now, who's to say it shouldn't be called love? (94)

Nadine Gordimer has underlined the struggle of the African people in her novels. In *The Late Bourgeois World* too, similar themes can be easily traced. However, a feminist reading of the novel convinces us of the extent of the debilitating sexism of the patriarchal society. The multiple social demands on a woman's life, and the referential climate of segregating the feminine from the masculine, giving unquestioned priority to the later, encourage social structures which compel a woman to opt for predefined choices only, by conditioning and thus controlling the very basis of her cognitive patterns. Through the character of Liz, *The Late Bourgeois World* touches upon the essential question of a woman's identity by delineating the psychic conflicts of personal origin and presenting the psychological strains of individual behaviour, underlining simultaneously the commonality of gender issues across cultural barriers, and the difficulty of transcending them completely in order to attain an autonomous selfhood.

NOTES

1. E.G. Burrows, Gordimer's interview, *Michigan Quarterly Review*, Vol. 9, no. 4, Fall 1970, pp. 231-39.
2. *Ibid.*
3. Nadine Gordimer and Lionel Abrahams, ed., *South African Writing Today* (Harmondsworth: Penguin, 1967), p. 6.
4. Nadine Gordimer, Nobel Lecture, 'Writing and Being,' December 7, 1991. *http://gos.sbc.edu/g/gordimer.html*
5. *Ibid.*
6. Per Wastberg, "Nadine Gordimer and South African Experience," *http://nobleprize.org/literature/articles/wastberg*
7. Joya F. Uraizee, "This is no Place for a Woman: Nadine Gordimer, Nayantara Sahgal, Buchi Emecheta, and the Politics of Gender," Trenton: African World Press 2000, *Amazon.com/ogp/reader/ 085654376Xref=sib_bc/102-4665760-8580153?5Fencoding=UTF &P=S00k # reader_page*
8. Elizabeth Cowie et al., "Representation vs. Communication," Mary Eagleton, ed., *Feminist Literary Theory: A Reader* (Second Edition, U.S.A.: Blackwell, 2001), p.164.
9. Simone de Beauvoir, *The Second Sex*, trans. H.M. Parshley (Great Britain: Vintage, 1991), p. 148.
10. Susan Sontag, "Against Interpretation," David Lodge, ed., *Twentieth Century Literary Criticism* (U.S.A.: Longman, 1972), p. 653.
11. Ruth Parkin-Gourelas, "What Isn't There" in Margaret Atwood's *The Blind Assassin*: The Psychoanalysis of Duplicity," *Modern Fiction Studies*, 50-3, Fall 2004, p. 682.
12. *Ibid*, p. 697.
13. Rachel Alsop, et al. *Theorizing Gender* (U.S.A.: Blackwell, 2002), p. 66.
14. Simone de Beauvoir, p. 450.

Michael Ondaatje's *The English Patient*: A Comprehensive Study

SANTWANA HALDAR
F.M. Auto. College, Balasore

An immigrant from Sri Lanka in Canada, Michael Ondaatje settled in Toronto and won fame for his poetic and narrative gifts. His collections of poems *The Collected Works of Billy and Kid: Left Handed Poems* (1970), *There's a Trick with a Knife I'm Learning to Do: Poems 1963-78* (1979) and *The Cinnamon Peeler: Selected Poems* (1991) secured his place as an established Canadian poet of the late twentieth century. But his universal fame is mostly due to his fictional writings which include *Coming through Slaughter* (1976), *Running in the Family* (1982), *In the Skin of a Lion* (1987) and *The English Patient* (1992) In *Running in the Family*, Ondaatje recorded the life of colonial Ceylon as experienced in his own family. The island Sri Lanka which in different historical periods, acquired different names such as Serendip, Ratnadipa, Taprobane, Zeloan, Ceylon etc., was invaded by different European nations—the Portuguese, the Dutch, and the English. Some outsiders, like the ancestors of Ondaatje himself, came to the island as professionals and settled there marrying Sinhalese women. The writer's thorough knowledge of history and his apprehension of the human values that shape history were widely appreciated. The extraordinary story of the building of Toronto in *In the Skin of a Lion* brought Ondaatje an international fame, but *The English Patient*, the first Canadian novel to have been rewarded the prestigious Booker Prize, is considered to be his best. The present article aims at a comprehensive study of *The English Patient* in which Ondaatje examined the movements of cultures in the twentieth century—the Western, Eastern, African and the

Bedouin culture as well—and painted sombre pictures of the post-World War horror and of colonial aggression, and wove a fascinating texture of exciting images including delicate erotic scenes.

The English Patient has an epigram at the beginning, before the chapters start, and it is a quotation from the minutes of the Geographical Society meeting held in London during some time in the nineteen forties. It runs as follows:

> Most of you, I am sure, remember the tragic circumstances of the death of Geoffrey Clifton at Gilf Kebir followed later by the disappearance of his wife Katharine Clifton, which took place during the 1939 desert expedition in the search of Zerzura. I cannot begin this meeting tonight without referring very sympathetically to these tragic occurrences.

The Acknowledgement at the end of the book clearly says that some of the characters in this book are based on historical figures, and that the Gilf Kebir and its surrounding desert were explored in the 1930s. The book is yet a fiction, the writer stresses, having imaginary characters and events.[1]

Reference to the tragic occurrences in the desert, as is found in the lines from the minutes of the Geographic society, apparently has little to do in the first three chapters, 'The Villa,' 'In Near Ruins' and 'Sometimes a Fire.' These three chapters project the background—the post-World War period near Florence in Italy—and suggest peculiar relationships among four persons, all shell-shocked and secluded, taking refuge in a nunnery turned into a hospital, evacuated at the time of war. It is the war that becomes more prominent than the characters in the novel. For it is the war that has brought them together. The first chapter introduces the central characters, the burnt man known as the English patient and his nurse Hana in the devastated villa San Girolamo. The patient was a mine of information but could not tell his own name. He was supposed to be a pilot whose plane was smashed in the desert. He had been brought to Siwa Oasis by the Bedouin and was hospitalized by the Allies. The second chapter introduces Caravaggio, the man with bandaged hands who had been in the military hospital in Rome for more than four months. He had been taking regular doses of morphine for the pain in his hands. When Caravaggio learnt of the English patient and his nurse, he came to join them in that terrible place where the last vices of war were still visible. "Dead cattle, Horses shot dead, half eaten, people hanging upside down from bridges." (29) It is revealed that Caravaggio was an old friend of Hana's father Patrick. During the war Caravaggio acted as a spy for the Allies; he was caught one night and both his thumbs were cut off. When hospitalized in Rome, Caravaggio hardly talked to anyone. But after he came to the villa he regained his early self. He felt that Hana had been overpowered with sadness and became obsessed with the patient who was almost dead. The third chapter introduces the fourth character, Kirpal Singh, the Sikh sapper from India, a member of the British army. He was entrusted with the duty of finding out hidden mines left by the retreating army. One stormy night he approached the villa, not out of curiosity about the sound of piano which was being played by Hana, but with an apprehension of a danger to the piano player. The retreating army often left pencil mines within musical instruments. Returning owners opened up pianos and lost their hands. After his arrival in the villa he seemed casually content with the small group of three persons. It was like a holiday for him "after the war of mud and rivers and bridges," and he entered the house only when invited in. He began to stay in a tent near the villa and was engaged in finding out mines in the garden. He had a transistor set that supplied him with the news of the outer world. And he would often pass on important information to Hana and Caravaggio.

The magnificent plot of the novel is woven out of the developments of complicated relationships among these four characters and the gradual revelations of their past through remembrances. Hana had lost her unborn child and its father in war and her father also died in war. She had been working as a nurse in the hospitals that were shell-shocked. During this time when she became friendless and homeless, she came across the English patient who looked like a burned animal, taut and dark (41).

Months later he became her last patient in the villa, and she refused to return with the others to the safety of the Pisa hospitals. She was warned of the uncleared mines, lack of water and food, but could not be persuaded to leave the place. The patient who could not remember his identity, was a wise man with a vast knowledge and was a saint for Hana. Caravaggio rightly observed that Hana was obsessed with her love for the burnt patient, and he tried to divert Hana's attention towards the young Sapper. But it was perhaps beyond Caravaggio's understanding that the dying man's relationship with Hana did not develop any aversion to life in her mind. Rather Hana became acquainted with the whole spectrum of life through reading aloud the texts as directed by the patient. Towards the end of the novel it is revealed that when the patient saw her for the first time, he understood her mental condition and sought to bring her back to normalcy through the bliss of great literature. It is also learnt towards the end of the book that Hana's father had died of the burn in war and Hana remained obsessed with the feeling that she could at least attend him in his sick bed as she was an expert in treating burn injury, if not cure him. Seen from this feeling towards her father, the patient seems to have been associated with the father image in her mind, and she did not like to part from him. Her decision to put off her uniform also symbolizes that she was not thinking herself to be a nurse.

As Hana read one book after another, following the instruction of the patient, she developed an urge for life. Her attempts to plant beans in one corner of the wild garden, suspected to be a hiding place for unexplored mines, suggest her newfound zeal.

"In spite of the burned earth, in spite of the lack of water. Someday there would be a bower of limes, rooms of green light." (43) As Hana went on reading books she experienced to have walked through the landscape described in the book. She travelled with the old wanderer in *Kim* or with Fabrizio in *The Charterhouse of Parma*. The book intoxicated the reader and the listener "in a swirl of armies and horses and wagons—those running away from or running towards a war." (93) The patient asked her to read Kipling slowly, taking pauses at the commas.

He gave a lesson about Kipling (94). Hana knew that if he slept in the middle of the reading, he need not worry, for the portion had been known to him earlier. Turning from the delisage and holy sentences at the end of *Kim*, she picked up the patient's note. Thin papers from the copy of a Bible were glued into the test. She wondered how he had managed to carry the book with him out of the fire. Thus instead of consoling her through his words, the patient chose a more fruitful path, that of showing life through the great classics and the process acted perfectly on her.

As Hana's mind was now fully prepared to understand love as a liberating force, she was drawn quite naturally, towards Kirpal Singh. At the beginning it was, however, Kirpal Singh who was torn by a desire to touch her when she sat watching the patient.

> If he could walk the seven yards across The Englishman's room and touch her he would be sane. (72)
> She put her fingers to her lips as he entered and then pointed to the patients. If he could walk across the room and touch her he would be sane. But between them lay a treacherous and complete journey. (113)
> If she had been reading or if she had been bending over the Englishman, he would have nodded to her and probably left, but he is now watching Hana as someone young and alone. To-night, gazing at the scene of the mine blast, he had begun to fear her presence during the afternoon dismantling. He had to remove it, or she would be with him each time he approached a fuse. (114)

And finally,

> He turns and pauses beside the bed. As the English patient completes one of his long exhalations he snips the wire of his hearing aid with the cutters and drops them back into the stached. He turns and grins towards her. (115)

Their union gave them a sense of security and sanity. They started having sound sleep when they remained together. As they grew intimate at night the space between them during the day grew larger. She liked the distance he left her. It gave each of them a private energy. Sometimes he passed a plate or some food into her hands, or she placed a leaf across his brown wrist. Or they would work with Caravaggio between them mortaring up a collapsing wall. Theirs was no possessive love. For Hana, in particular, love was an existentialist's choice, a free act that could not be obligatory. When she crossed two hundred yards of dark garden to reach his tent she might find him sleeping. But she knew that it was not from his lack of love but from necessity. On his part, Kip loved the whole of Hana, and he liked her most as she crawled against his body "like a saint." (122)

Peculiarly, yet, Hana felt that Caravaggio would explain to her how she could sink into love. (130) Hana's love for Kip was not exclusive. She needed the presence of both Caravaggio and the patient for fulfilling the world of her love gradually, both Caravaggio and Kip got more and more attached to the patient. Kip liked what he called an abstract madness of autodidactic in the patient, and often sat beside him to listen to his wisdom. It seemed to Hana to be a reversal of Kipling's *Kim*, The young student was now Indian, the wild old teacher, English.

This interweaving of relationships could hardly contribute to the movement of the plot. Caravaggio's search for the identity of the patient and the Hiroshima Nagasaki incident are the two issues that caused the necessary movement. A new element is introduced in the fourth chapter. It is all about the desert expeditions. The British Royal Geographical Society founded in 1830, promoted exploration in Australia, Africa and the Arctic. In early twentieth century its expeditions were extended to Asia and the Antarctic. The fourth chapter entitled 'South Cairo 1930-1938' gives details of the expeditions of the African Desert through the patient's reminiscences. In 1930, the patient recalled, they had begun mapping the greater part of the Gilf Kebir Plateau, looking for the lost Oasis Zerzura which had been known as the Oasis of little Birds or the City of Acacias, or The White City, Seven explorers had come to the place: Kemel el Din came in 1925, Bagnold during 1930-32 Almasy-Madox during 1931-37. As the patient remembered, they were a small clutch of a nation between the wars, mapping and exploring. They gathered at Dakhla and Kufra as if those were bars or cafes. Giving details of their expeditions which were directly taken from the archival material and the geographical Journals[2] the patient remarked,

> There were rivers of desert tribes, the most beautiful humans. . . . We were German, English, Hungarian, African—all of us insignificant to them. Gradually we became nationless. I came to hate nations. We are deformed by nation states. The desert could not be claimed or owned—it was a piece of cloth carried by winds, never held down by stores, and given a hundred shifting names long before Canterbury existed, long before battles and treaties quilted Europe and the East. All of us . . . wished to remove the clothing of our countries. It was a place of faith. We disappeared into landscape. (118-19)

The deist, yet, could not be set aside during the war. The strategic value of the desert being important to all the military powers, the desert became the spot of direct fighting. And the patient regretted, "This was a world that had been civilized for centuries, had a thousand paths and roads" (140)

The fifth chapter entitled 'Katharine' depicts the patient's love affair with a married lady. In the sixth chapter Caravaggio said to Hana that he suspected the patient to be a Hungarian named Almasy who worked for the German during the war in 1930s. He had been a great desert explorer and had helped map the Sand sea. In 1941 he became a guide for spies, taking them across the desert into Cairo. With this suspicion uttered by Caravaggio, the plot is given a flair of suspense.

Caravaggio continued his search, applying more doses of morphine to the patient when he was not catching everything, his love affair or the death of his friend Madox, for example. The plot becomes a net of spell binding revelations of facts and dreams, of thrilling adventures and passionate love. The patient, yet, did not admit that he was Almasy, though he sometimes spoke in the third person referring to Almasy and sometimes in the first person. When Caravaggio wanted to know whether the third person was he himself the patient quoted: "Death means you are in the third person." Finally, in the chapter entitled 'The Cave of Swimmers,' the epigraph quoted at the beginning of the book gets linked to the story. It is learnt that Geoffrey Clifton, who belonged to the British Intelligence and who had joined the Almasy-Madox expedition during 1931-37 as an amateur, was actually spying on the group as the desert was being controlled by the armies during the war. The tragic death of Clifton was due to a plane crash in which his wife Katharine was also severely injured. Almasy, who had been in deep love with Katharine, was waiting for the arrival of the couple in the desert. After the plane crash it was Almasy who rescued the dead body of Clifton and took the injured body of Katharine to the cave of swimmers. She needed nursing, medicine and food. Leaving her in the cave, Almasy went out for seeking help. His hope to get any vehicle being denied, he walked for three days without food. Then at El Taj, he was arrested by the English military personnel who refused to listen to his story of the woman injured at Uweinat seventy miles away. It was because he described her as his wife and not as Mrs. Clifton, that no one listened to him.

> They were using these wicker prisons size of a shower. I was put into one and moved by truck. I was flailing around in there until I fell off into the street, still in it. I was yelling Katharine's name. Yelling the gilf Kebir. Whereas the only name I should have yelled, was Clifton's. They hauled me up into the truck again. I was just another possible second-rate spy. Just another international bastard. (251)

The Allied troops spied over his activities and he could not go near Uweinat. Then he went over to the Germans, guiding the German spies into Cairo. And when at last he could manage to enter the cave of swimmers he found her whole body covered in bright pigments. Her body seemed to him to be a work of cartography marked by nature, by herbs, stones and the ash of acacia. The disappearance of Katharine Clifton, which is referred to in the epigraph at the beginning of the novel, is thus made out not as fact, but as fiction.

A perfect blending of fact and fiction, in the background of desert world which is both physical and imaginative, forms the "Magic carpet" of the plot which, as says Pico Iyer, "soars across world and times."[3]

Besides the revelation of the patient's identity it was the incident of dropping atom bomb on the two Japanese cities, Hiroshima and Nagasaki, that brought a turning point to the plot through Kirpal Singh's discovery of his own colonial reality. Kip had earlier told Hana repeatedly that he did not share his brother's attitude to the British against whom he was struggling in India. But the Hiroshima-Nagasaki incident brought an outright change in his attitude to the British and he developed hatred towards the colonial power. Led by this hatred he even went to shoot at the burnt man who was known as the English patient. He now understood that the colonial power had compelled him and a million of Asian youths to join the war. Even after Caravaggio explained that the patient was a Hungarian who acted against the Allies, his anger was not appeased. The patient as an individual was not his target; it was the aggression of the colonial powers that mattered. The British, he argued, somehow converted the rest of the world as they were universally accepted as representatives of perfect customs and perfect manners. This submissive attitude of the Asians, he felt, had helped the British to exploit the Asians. Kirpal Singh said to the patient.

> You and then the Americans converted us. With your missionary rules. And Indian soldiers wasted their lives as heroes so they could be pukkah. You had wars like cricket" (283)

He continued,

> American, French, I don't care. When you start bombing the brown races of the world, you're an Englishman. You had king Leopold of Belgium and now you have fucking Harry Truman of the U.S.A. You all learned it from the English. (284)

Caravaggio also thought that the Sikh soldier was right, that they would never have dropped such a bomb on a white nation. Kirpal Singh was so much obsessed with the Atom bomb that when he closed his eyes he saw fire; he saw people keeping into rivers and reservoirs to avoid flame or heat that could burn everything within seconds. He was astonished with the thought that the "brilliant" bomb was carried over the sea in a plane and was then released on the Island. Though he had been dealing with small bombs, he knew nothing about that weapon called Atom bomb. He did not know whether it was a sudden assault of metal and explosion or if boiling air scoured itself towards human beings. He could no more tolerate the rude shock and left the place. He apprehended a new war and the death of human civilization itself. So long Kip remained in the make-believe world he was loyal to the British Raj. But the single incident of dropping Atom bombs disillusioned him. His newly developed Asian identity led him to abandon Italy and go back to his homeland Punjab.

> He was travelling against the direction of the invasion, as if rewinding the spool of war, the route no longer tense with military. He took only roads he knew, seeing the familiar caste towns from a distance. . . . He carried little, all weapons left behind. The bike hurled through each village, not slowing for town or memory of war. (290)

During his journey he tried his best not to think of Hana.

> Everything he saw through the goggles was grey. He would not think of Hana. In all the silence within the bike's noise he did not think of her. (293)

He kept Hana away from his mind but it seemed to him that he was carrying, the body of the Englishman with him in that flight. The desert image merged with the image of devastation caused by Atom Bomb in his consciousness. "A secrèt of deserts from Uweinat to Hiroshima." (295) While riding speedily Kirpal Singh suddenly fell down in the water, "the metal body between his legs as they slammed into it, jarring a white path through it, disappearing, the rain too entering the river." (295) This sudden dramatic turn adds the final suspense to the story. However, the novel ends with the sapper, settled in India as a doctor with a happy family and opening the "trigger of memory" to reach the villa in Florence. He visualized Hana as if revealed through a camera's film. Recalling the time, he was just as fascinated at himself there as he was with her. It was her character, her effort to assert her individuality that impressed him, and he could never forget her. Every month or two he saw her as if in a vision, as if those moments of revelation were "a continuation of the letters she wrote to him for a year, getting no reply, until she stopped sending them, turned away by his silence." (300) The novel ends with an image of Hana as visualized by Kip.

> She is a woman of honour and smartness whose wild love leaves out luck, always taking risks, and there is something in her brow now that only she can recognize in a mirror. Ideal and idealistic in that shiny dark hair! (301)

Such an ending reveals an extraordinary poetic quality, a rare one, particularly in the post war scenario.

It is above all the exciting images in the novel that explain the success of its cinematographic version directed by Walter Minghella. The novel starts with one such image: the tall swaying cypresses in the garden producing a buckle of noise in the air startle the only female character on the scene who feels the first drops of rain on her bare arms, and then enters the villa in darkness. She enters a room, the walls and ceilings of which are filled up with paintings of trees and a man is seen lying on the bed with his burnt body. Stephen Scobie rightly observed that it is typical that Ondaatje would begin his book with an image rather than a character or a plot.[4] This image making capacity shows that his sensibility as a writer is grounded in poetry and that all his novels may be described as poetic novels. The distinctness of the images used by Ondaatje lies in the fact that his images are not burdens on the plot, but rather they help the plot move forward. Take, for example, the Hiroshima image. The repeated use of the image highlights the logic behind the radical change in Kip—his attempt to shoot the patient and his sudden flight. At the same time, the particular image reveals that the anti-war text is interpreted through their experiences.

Among the texts used in *The English patient* for intertextual references, there are Herodotus' *Histories*, Stendhal's *The Charter House of Parma* and Kipling's *Kim*. The patient had added his personal notes, drawings and maps to the Histories, and his own interpretations of history and geography are better expressed through the quotations from Herodotus. Herodotus dealt with Egyptian legends and the patient's task was to go on an expedition for searching the lost Oasis Zerzura. Only a man of vast knowledge, as Almasy had been, can correlate different branches of knowledge to arrive at wisdom. *The Charter House of Parma* that deals with Napoleon's invasion of Italy has also been quoted profusely. Of all the texts Kipling's *Kim* has been used most effectively. The young English man in Kipling's novel is the counterpoint to the sapper, Kirpal Singh nicknamed Kip by his friends in London. The British boy in *Kim* immerses himself in the Indian way of life sitting at the feet of the Buddhist monk. In Ondaatje's novel it is reversed, the young man being an Indian youth who listened to the wisdom of the patient supposed to be Englishman. The phonic similarities between Kim, Kip and Kipling have also drawn the critics' attention.[6]

As an anti-war novel *The English Patient* has been equated to *All Quiet on the Western Front*, and other such internationally famous books. During the time of war falsehood prevails in every walk of life. 'Lie' and 'Ownership' are detected as two vices behind the war. (152) It is the rich who declare war (123), Caravaggio points out:

> The trouble with all of us is we are where we should not be. What are we doing in Africa, in Italy? What is Kip doing dismantling bombs in Orchards, for God's sake? What is he doing fighting English wars? (122)

One is reminded of T.S. Eliot's poem "To the Indians who Died in Africa."

> A man's destination is his own village, . . .
> This was not your land, or ours but a village in the Midlands,
> And one in The Five Rivers, may have the same graveyard.
> Let those who go home tell the same story of you:
> Of action with a common purpose, action
> None the less fruitful if neither you nor we
> Know, until the judgement after death,
> What is the fruit of action.

The most distinctive quality of *The English Patient* lies, however, in a perfect blending of dissimilar things: details of the constructions of Bomb and the description time of the British

Bomb Disposal units at the start of world war go side by side with the stories of passionate love. Besides the Kip-Hana couple there are Almasy and Katharine, though the latter's presence is felt only through Almasy's consciousness. Both these couples enjoyed intensely passionate experiences and also suffered the pangs of the tragic end of romance. The height of imaginative flight fits in with the realistic descriptions in the chapter 'In Situ' which are directly taken from *Unexploded Bomb* by Major A.B. Hartley.[7]

The writer's use of symbols has added a special chain to the novel. The search for the oasis Zerzura in the African desert may symbolize a search for love in the post-World War desert. The novel may be called 'The Waste Land' in prose, composed of images taken from the war-torn world. Finally, the riveting beauty of Ondaatje's language arrests the readers' attention. The art of magical storytelling used in a thought-provoking novel deserves a secure place in English literature.

NOTES

1. *The English Patient* (Picador, 1992), p. 305.
2. Qtd. back cover of the novel.
3. Stephen Scobie, 'The Reading Lesson: Michael Ondaatje and the Patients of Desire,' *Essays on Canadian Writing* (1994), p. 93.
4. Peter Verdonk and Jean Jacques Weber, eds. *Twentieth Century Fiction: From Text to Context* (London: Routledge, 1995), p. 248
5. Paula Garcia-Ramiry, 'The Colonial Context of Michael Ondaatje's *The English Patient*,' *The Atlantic Literary Review*, Vol. 12, p. 47.

Margaret Atwood's *The Edible Woman*: A Quest for Positive Identity and Spiritual Survival

UDAY SHANKAR OJHA
Jagdam College, Chapra

Over nearly thirty years during which Margaret Atwood has published ten novels, ten books of poetry and three short story collections, she has shown tremendous talent for surprising her readers with her ongoing experimentalism and her radical challenges to contemporary social and cultural myths and fashionable ideologies. The oeuvres of this superb creationist have "contributed substantially to the definition of a national identity in Canadian literature and to its international reputation, signposting a specific landscape and culture as an important location in the 'global village.'"[1]

Margaret Atwood stands as one of the pioneers of contemporary Canadian women's fiction in English today and rightly deserves the most coveted Booker award bestowed upon her for her novel. A celebrity of the millennium year, Atwood earned global reputation because of her debut novel *The Edible Woman* (1969) which became the epoch-making voice owing to her abiding and presiding commitment for women's identity, the layers and levels of consciousness in a male chauvinistic society and the myriad meanings of men-women encounter. This paper, however, intends to analyze and examine the struggle of the characters in *The Edible Woman* to overcome alienation, their quest for positive identity and spiritual survival in "the seemingly sane but actually insane society which is both predatory and suffocatingly sexist."[2]

Before diving into the depth of the text and texture of the novel itself, the problem of a unique Canadian identity which has further been complicated by the country's preference for a 'mosaic' rather than a 'melting pot' structure, needs to be briefly explained. Canadian national identity still remains as elusive as ever on account of its being an economic colony of the United States and emergence of small, isolated, closely-knit garrison societies of the French-Canadians and English-Canadians in which moral and social values are deemed unquestionable. The "Colonial Cringe" imprinted "almost like genetic information" on the Canadian sensibility has adversely affected the slow and painful psychological transition of Canada from a colóny to a nation. As in most postcolonial cultures, the Canadian experience of an acute identity crisis, though as a temporary amnesia caused by the country's subordinate position under imperial overloads has made "survival" the great fact of Canadian life.

Since "nations are to a large extent invented by their poets and novelists,"[3] the protagonists of mainstream writers like Atwood, Laurence, Kroetsch and Hodgins struggle hard to transcend the wilfully cast victim state of the Canadians. Margaret Atwood's *The Edible Woman*, particularly, reflects her strong disapproval of the negative identity which emerges from the self-destructive survival myth. Throughout the novel, Marian MacAlpin, Atwood's "abnormally normal" heroine is involved in the exciting process of fostering a more positive identity very much in tune with the spirit of postmodernism for the desire for a 'single,' 'unified' spiritual identity. Her struggle to overcome alienation and achieve personal and social integration is "imagined as a freedom to love, to share, to meet, to touch such a state which is our spiritual home, the human goal the grail."[4] However, Atwood strongly asserts to the Irving Layton's stand that "every artist is an incurable mythologist"[5] and advocates first for the need for vital communal myths to fill up the spiritual void created by the erosion of religious faith in modern western technological society in general and secondly the need for personal myths to help overcome feelings of alienation and despair in particular. In the theoretical framework of the text, Atwood embraces and devoutly diagnoses that the quest for spiritual survival depends on rejecting the mythos created for consumers and re-discovering the world of myth. A close adherence to the indigenous myths, religion and culture and an outright rejection of the habit to importing religion and culture from other countries are the most obvious and recurrent episodes inhibited in the other novels also like Atwood's *Surfacing* and Margaret Laurence's *The Diviners*.

Emerging from the vortex of the theoretical framework of the novel, if we focus our attention to the very epigraph of *The Edible Woman*, which is the recipe for puff pastry from I.S. Robauer and M.R. Becker's *The Joy of Cooking*, we find that "the novel itself with its light, witty and effervescent tone is a kind of puff pastry but also that a certain amount of pain is involved in the making of good puff pastry as the fingers of the one who makes it "should be chilled throughout the operation."[6] Like three other novels, this novel is also set in the city of Toronto. The city, though described realistically, often takes on mythic overtones and functions as a potent symbol of identity crisis in the world at large. A profound sense of rootlessness is sensed throughout the novel particularly in the images like boarding houses, rented rooms and hotels.

The Edible Woman is considered to be a manifesto of post-colonial women sensibility and sensitivity where states of marginality and 'otherness' are seen as sources of energies for potential change and progress. The writer, in fact, becomes the creator of reality and explores the themes like victimization and survival. The question of female identity, the politics of gender—alienation of women in a male dominated society, the narrow de-limiting definition of a woman and her function in society and man's attempt to destroy the selfhood of women are some other vibrating inquiries which run like a red thread throughout the novel. As a reaction to this, we see a gradual carrying out of female spaces through various strategies, and her quest for identity, self-definition and autonomy.

Atwood's *Survival*, her thematic guide to Canadian literature, categorizes woman in four basic 'victim' positions, which not only helps us to explore the various possibilities available but it also indicates a way out of this gender power struggle. The three female characters Lucy, Millie and Emmy, whom Ainsley collectively calls "the office virgins," actively hunt for husbands. At the party, they waste no time when they spot Leonard as single and available. The conventional role of women as wife, sexual object and their availability is explored in these characters when they get Leonard "backed against the wall in the neuter area now, two of them on the sides cutting off flank escape and the third in front" while Emmy and Millie are fairly dumb and hunt occasionally. Lucy is clever and cunning and is constantly on the prowl. With her "delicious dresses and confectionary eyes"[7] she trails herself "like a many-plumed fish-lure with glass beads and three spinners and seventeen hooks through the likely-looking places, good restaurants and cocktail bars . . . where the right kind of men might be expected to be lurking, ravenous as pike, though more martially inclined." (112)

Contrary to this first category of women like Emmy, Lucy and Millie who seem to be completely brainwashed by this more glamourized rendering of the slogan "biology is destiny" and wish to be happy suburban housewives, Clara, a wife and mother of three, is a suburban housewife but is far from being happy. Embarrassed by her "mental grey-out,"[8] Clara seems to be undergoing an identity crisis. Realizing the hoax played on women like her by their society who daren't voice their unease and resign to a life of matrimony and motherhood, Clara, to her husband Joe, "allows her core to get taken over by the husband. And when the kids come, she makes up one morning and discovers she doesn't have anything left inside, she's hollow, she doesn't know who she is any more, her core has been destroyed." (236) Now, this is the second stage of victimization; the woman acknowledges the fact of being a victim but accepts it as something inevitable.

Ainsley, a dynamic, action-oriented rebellious graduate in psychology, is just the opposite of Clara. She repudiates the victim role. She subverts the traditional male-female victim predator role assumptions and exploits man to fulfill her needs. She decides to have a baby sans the encumbrance of a legal husband because, according to the 'experts,' "Every woman should have at least one baby. . . . It's even more important than sex. It fulfills your deepest feminity." (40-41) Turning into "a scheming superfemale," (122) she hunts for a male with healthy genes to impregnate her succumbing ultimately to flamboyant playboy Len's weakness for young and inexperienced girls. Ainsley's dream that her child will be a boy is almost shattered when she is told by a male psychologist that in the absence of a strong Father Image in the home, boys often tend to be homosexuals. Lastly, Ainsley's being blessed with fertility worshipper fish and her fall into matrimony reflect the hypocritical stand of feminine mystique in the North American society.

Atwood, very subtly but implicitly, makes out a case against each of these possible alternatives that Marian can either choose to be the 'scheming superwoman' like Ainsley, or the submissive 'earth mother' Clara or the opportunistic 'office virgins.' In this connection, Alan Jawe, in the introduction to the novel, opines: "*The Edible Woman* is a novel about choices." Marian is not a static figure, she moves through the three positions till she arrives at the fourth, i.e., becoming a creative non-victim. Analyzing Marian's psychological journey away from her society and back to it, Coomi S. Vevaina critically examines the "mythological overtones" present in it and finds that "Marian's regression from a conventional-minded adult to a foetus and her development from a foetus to an unconventional adult reveal her struggle for spiritual survival in Crazyland." (114) At the beginning of the novel, Marian appears to be a 'normal' and 'well-adjusted' young woman who compliments herself on her "moral superiority" to Ainsley. Marian doesn't believe in the absurdity of Emmy, Lucy and Millie also, who vehemently desire to trap husbands into matrimony rather considers herself and Peter, infinitely superior to Clara and Poe who "aren't practical enough, and have no sense at all of how to run a well organized marriage." (102) It is nothing but a vague acceptance of the victim role. With her engagement to Peter, she gradually loses her autonomy and becomes increasingly dependent on him. This loss of autonomy and self-identity is accompanied by a loss of appetite physically and the loss of the 'first person singular' voice in the narrative structure. The more she conforms to Peter's standards, the more violently "her body rejects various kinds of foods." (177) It is the consumer society which encourages its victim to passively consume rather than actively create.

The predatory side of Marian finds its fullest manifestation in her desire to play the role of a nurse. "The embryonic noble nurse that is supposed to be curled, efficient and self sacrificing in the heart of every true woman" (109) is rather active in Marian.

The state of growing uncertainty aggravates further the quest for identity and it is conveyed through the reflections she snaps of herself in various objects. "The small silvery image" of her "upside down reflection" indicates her mental status in a state of flux. When having a bath, she sees "a curiously-sprawling pink thing" (218) in the hot and cold taps and the spout between them. However, it is worth noticing that Marian's alienation is the direct outcome of her passivity also.

Marian's quest for individuation and selfhood brings her back to cling to the only one self-image left to her; that of a nurse. But to her utter dismay and depression, when she asks Duncan how he feels being initiated into sex the previous night, he ruthlessly replies: "You want me to say it was stupendous, don't you? . . . That it got me out of my shell. Hatched me into manhood. Solved all my problems. . . . It was fine; just as good as usual." (264)

Now, this is alarming. Marian's marriage to Peter would be disastrous to her own integrity. On the other hand, Duncan's awkward and wayward response to her is a painful realization. She comes to know that she is not the first and "the starched nurse-like image of herself she had tried to preserve as a last resort crumpled like wet newsprint." (264) Like the narrator of *Surfacing*, she seems to be caught in a violent duality and refuses to be a victim. She wants to reclaim her body and reinscribe it with different meanings of power, action and strength. When she regains her identity, her body (stomach) is restored to its former equilibrium and she finds her voice again. The narrative goes back to the first person to imply a rediscovery of the self.

Through the character of Marian, Atwood has exhibited that a woman will be consumed if she projects herself as an 'edible' object. In a crystallized structured form, Atwood "successfully makes way for the new woman not as a consumer product in a capitalistic society but a woman transforming the marginal experiences into a creative force and potent energy."[9]

Uptil now, the focus of this paper has been on the female characters of this novel but one can't disagree with John Lauber who in his well researched paper clear-sightedly notes that male and female identity are equally problematic "and the novel insistently asks whether and how anyone can achieve identity in the artificial society"[10] in which we all live.

In *The Edible Woman,* Peter is the most tragically self-alienated male character who is unaware of his true inner self. "Peter-the-Presentable" is a lawyer and even with a small firm "he is rising in it like a balloon." (17) Symbolical of his being made up of surfaces and totally without a core, to reveal his masculinity, he keeps two rifles, a pistol and "several wicked-looking knives" (59) on a pegboard in his bedroom. Moreover, he decides to marry Marian for she appears the most "sensible" (64, 89) of all the women he knows. "Sensible" is synonymous with "conventional" for Peter, who along with Len, feels self-alienated due to the masculine mystique created by the frustrations and anxieties of the sick society. Marian suits his taste for her passivity and her lack of strong convictions and feels she is not the kind of girl who would try to "take over his life." (61) But very soon, Marian feels the predatory side of Peter who regards her as a thing rather than as a person. This feeling, in fact, of being ruled over and measured before being spiritually slaughtered, severs her engagement with Peter.

Though Peter thinks of himself as entirely 'normal' for the majority of people around him seem to think and act like him, he is trying his best to come out of the vortex of continuing alienation from the inner self.

However, *The Edible Woman* in the critical and theoretical perspective truly pronounces the concept of "power politics." It is nothing but the bifurcation of reality into hostile opposites, which permits the patterns of subordination and domination. Here, the most vital statistics is "how power operates and who has power over whom."[11] But ultimately the unconscious part of the psyche, which alone apprehends the world of myth, brings back the vision of life, in its own way to the characters. Since myths are "clues to the spiritual potentialities of human life,"[12] they help create a deeper awareness of life itself and facilitate a way for inner journey leading to the quest for positive identity and spiritual survival.

NOTES

1. Coomi s. Vevaina, *Re/membering Selves: Alienation and Survival in the Novels of Margaret Atwood and Margaret Laurence* (Creative, New Delhi, 1996), foreword.
2. *Ibid.*, p. 102.
3. Aldous Huxley, *Texts and Pretexts* (New York: 1993), pp. 51-52.
4. Patricia Morley, "The Long Trek Home: Margaret Laurence's Stories," *Journal of Canadian Studies*, 11, No. 4 (November 1976), p. 19.
5. Clara Thomas, "A Conversation about Literature: An Interview with Margaret Laurence and Irving Layton," *Journal of Canadian Fiction*, 1, No. 1 (Winter 1972), p. 67.
6. Coomi S. Vevaina, *Re/membering Selves*, p. 102.
7. Margaret Atwood, *The Edible Woman* (1969; rpt. London: Virago, 1984), p. 112.
8. Betty Friedan, *The Feminine Mystique* (1963: rpt. Middlesex: Penguin, 1983), p. 20.
9. Pushkala Shivram, "A Search for Identity in Atwood's *The Edible Woman*," *Literary Journal*, Vol. 21, March 1998 (Stella Maris College, Chennai), p. 17.
10. John Lauber, "Alice in Consumerland: The Self-Discovery of Marian MacAlpin," *The Canadian Novel: Here and Now*, ed. John Moss (Toronto: New Canadian Press, 1978), p. 20.
11. Coomi S. Vevaina, "A Conversation with Margaret Atwood," *Times of India*, Sunday Review Section, 20 March 1988, p. 8.
12. Bill Moyer's interview with Joseph Campbell (video tape), "The Message of Myth," Part II of *The Power of Myth* (Apastrophe S. Productions and Public Affairs Television, 1988).

Is Woman a Consumer-Product?: A Study of Margaret Atwood's *Lady Oracle*

G. DOMINIC SAVIO
The American College, Madurai

The ideology of globalization and consumerism subsists on two levels of enquiry. The first one is in relation to the general economic proposition that unlimited consumerism paves way for globalization. The other level of investigation is in relation to a metaphysical representation of consumerism. In an age of phallocentrism, the body of a woman becomes the biggest consumer product. Consistent and systematic exploitation of female body for the purpose of sexual gratification seems to sum up the age of phallocentric patriarchy.

Margaret Atwood's *Lady Oracle* may be conceived as a female kunstleroman revolting against the patriarchal practice by enlisting the body of a woman as a text for sexual gratification. The protagonist, Joan Forster, sees the evils of phallocentrism and patriarchy. Her experience is a symbol of universal experience of a woman becoming biggest consumer item. This process is treated by the novelist as commodization of woman. Basically, consumerism and commodization seem to be moving on, taking the body of a woman only as a product of physical consumption.

Atwood's *Lady Oracle* examines the pathetic condition of women as products of sexual consumerism. The main thesis of the novel is the novelist's objection to the reduction of woman as an object for sexual enjoyment. The phallocentric patriarchal tradition has treated procreation as a sacred ideal and woman as a companion of man is meant for this worthy ideal. This attitude of women being allied with the role of procreation leads to the conception of woman as a kind of biological unit. So the patriarchal tradition assigns and recognizes two roles of a woman,

woman as a spiritual unit and as a biological agent. There has been a tilt in the balance of the two roles and in course of time it undergoes a degeneration. So long as faith existed there was no reversal in the roles played by woman. The wretchedness of man is such that he refuses to regard woman as a living human partner in the life's transaction. With the disappearance of faith and values, the biological tint given in the patriarchal tradition for women is exploited. Therefore perverting the role of woman comes from the perversity in the character of men.

Atwood's attention in *Lady Oracle* is focussed upon the biological role which a woman is forced to play in the degenerate male-dominated society. This attitude of male chauvinism is inevitably bound up with the patriarchal phallocentric tradition which is endorsed by such people to justify the role of woman as an object for sexual gratification. It is defined in general Economics that the purpose of a commodity is to satisfy a want. Similarly on the basis of this analogy the purpose of a woman is to satisfy the sexual needs or wants of a man. The greater a commodity satisfies a want, the higher its utility. Correspondingly the greater a woman satisfies a man, the higher will be her utility. This attitude of utility-related and demand-channelised consumerism is affixed to the role of women. It is the evil mind of men which runs after the body of woman only for the purpose of securing biological fulfillment. This kind of thinking corrupts and cripples the society which places emphasis upon woman as packages for man's consumerism. This idea of consumerism comes from gender bias which, in turn, is associated with the male-dominated society.

Atwood's *Lady Oracle* is a scathing attack on the male-dominated society which has downgraded woman as a consumer package. This novel is a psychological and confessional record of the forced roles of women and the masks of costumed men. The life of the protagonist, Joan Foster, and her observations of her mother's tragedy and her foster-mother's life reveal how women are treated as objects of satisfaction of the consumerists. Joan comes to know from her mother that she is the outcome of unwanted pregnancy, carrying her sad story around her neck like the story of "a rotting albatross." (238)

Woman at the mercy of man seems to be the tragic lot. The experience of Joan Foster being tortured in the hands of wayward men is already attested by the experience of her mother's and foster-mother's tragedy. Joan Foster is pained to note that a woman does not enjoy a life of dignity and self-respect. She is a biological pumpkin or cabbage, an edible woman for the consumption of man.

Joan Foster's so-called father was an anaesthetist and healer-cum-killer. His interest was primarily in the body of Foster's mother. He never looked upon her as a woman bristling with life and consciousness. Foster's mother admits, "I had to make the best of a bad job." (82) Next comes the foster-mother of Joan Foster, Aunt Lou, whose gambler husband never treated her as a human being. She was nothing but a consuming item in the hands of her husband who was shot dead for not paying back the borrowed money. From these events, Foster comes to know the plight of woman being used as a consumer product. The unfortunate tragedy of her mother and the lonely life of Aunt Lou make Foster revolt against the patriarchal system, the very name in which every injustice done to woman is validated. All possibilities of a real life for woman are sapped by this system.

Joan Foster grows up under the care of Aunt Lou who is a Chief Publication Relation Officer in a firm in Canada. Her visit to the Canadian National Exhibition convinces her of the idea of woman as a consumer product when a fat-sized woman is seated on a tiny stool. The problem of livelihood is what drives this woman to this game in the exhibition. All the three women Joan has come across in life have no independent say in anything. What is good for them is decided by others. What is worse is the imposition of men's views on them. The first half of the novel depicts the suffering of these three women and the other half of the novel focuses on Joan Foster's experiences of disappointment with costumed men, pretenders and dissemblers, who intend to use her as a consumer product for their sexual satisfaction.

Joan Foster's life is a running commentary on the phenomenon of woman being used as a consumer product. She witnesses this fact in her relation with five different kinds of cheats and impostors. The first person to exploit Joan is the Italian cook when Foster works in Bite-A Bit restaurant. He offers a series of temptations in order to win her love. But his motive is not at all noble. His real selfish materialistic intention is easily discernible in his words, "I am serious. I want to meet with your father, and look. I show you my bank account." (109) He pushes a little blue bank book towards her and further says, " I will give you babies; lot of babies. I see you like the babies. You are a good girl." (109)

Foster realizes that this is nothing but an attempt at destroying the dignity of woman. The Italian cook does not possess the necessary frame of mind to realize that the Bank account and materialistic comfort can never be a perennial source of attraction for a woman. Instead of a psychological and spiritual tie-up, he prefers only materialistic comfort. Foster is shrewd enough to see that the Italian cook is a person who wants to secure satisfaction of biological urges through a strategy of offering materialistic comforts. She sees the attitude of man who aims at reducing woman to the degenerate state of a commodity. Marriage is a relationship and it can never become a commercial transaction.

Life is a trial disclosing unknown possibilities. One such moment appears in the life of Foster when she fells off a double-decker bus in London. It is during this accident she happens to see Paul who is a Polish Count, poses as "Mavis Quilp," the writer of Nurse novels. His novels reveal his dirty mind, highlighting the illegitimate sexual relations between doctors and nurses. Such a person is not suitable for Foster who looks upon him as a scheming manipulator. Moreover his estimate and conception of woman are perceived by Foster in the following lines:

> It is an odd term, "mistress" . . . that was how he thought of me; these were the categories into which his sexual life was arranged: wives and mistresses. I was not the first mistress. For him there was no such thing as a female lover. (167)

Foster dislikes Paul as he views woman as "empty vessels," visualizes them as child-bearers, regards them as mistresses, considers men superior to women and he treats women inferior in intellectual attainments. Above all she hates Paul for he believes, "the mystery of man is of the mind, whereas that of woman is of the body." (188) This ignoble view of woman as a consumer product threatens Foster and drives her away from Paul.

Life on earth is an adventure which throws human beings into peculiar relationships. One such testing moment in the life of Foster is when she chances to see Arthur. The leftist ideology of Arthur, his interest in civil rights and his active involvement in "ban-the-bomb movement" draw her close to him. She is unwisely trapped into a frigid, cold and lifeless marriage with Arthur. His view of marriage is ridiculous:

> Marriage itself would settle us down, and through it, too, we would be better acquainted. If it didn't work out, well, it would be a learning experience. Most importantly, we would like much more cheaply together than we could separately. (220)

Arthur's view of marriage as an expression of an economy of frugality horrifies Foster. His attitude that it is good to live not because it is really good to live but because it is cheap, is not acceptable to Foster. The sacred idea of marriage as procreation is not relished by Arthur who urges Joan to use birth-control devices and pills. Much against her will, she learns cooking to please him but his irresponsive and non-cooperative nature comes out in the words of Foster himself. "Arthur enjoyed my defeats. They cheered him up. . . . My failure was a performance and Arthur was the audience." (234-35)

The positive attitude of a husband is to appreciate even the failure of his wife and encourage her to rise anew with fresh efforts towards betterment. But Arthur was a sadist who enjoys all the more when Foster fails. Soon she discovers Arthur to be a man having multiple selves in him. His interest in Foster is not genuine because his interest in leftist ideology is not genuine. Foster is at a loss to know when Arthur holds up Marlene, a married woman, having illicit relation with Sam, the Assistant editor of the leftist magazine, *Resurgence* as a model of virtue. Foster does not accept Arthur because he does not accept woman as a being endowed with dignity.

Life on earth is not only a mystery but it is a tale told by an idiot carrying no meaning. This maxim comes true in the life of Foster when she develops an intimacy with Chuck, the Royal Porcupine. He is a perfect dissembler. At one time he appears as Chuck, the Royal Porcupine and at another time he appears as Chuck, the Brewer. His intention is to be a husband of Joan Foster at a tome when she has developed deep vexation with Arthur. He seduces Foster to leave Arthur. Chuck is unaware of Arthur's sadistic torture of Foster. But he raises a question unwittingly as to why Joan is placed in the predicament of leaving Arthur. Chuck's comment on Foster is characteristic of the intention as well as the inner motive of his plan to use woman as a sexual tool, "You are like an out-of-control school bus." (300) The sinister motive of Chuck is discovered by Joan at a time when Paul reappears on the scene in order to steal her away from Arthur:

> You can trust me. You were a child, you did not know your own mind. Now you are a woman. You will leave this man, you will divorce, we will be happy. . . . If you tell him it is I you love, he will. . . . But I have friends. If necessary I shall steal you. (312)

Every man uses Joan Foster and leaves her as soon as his sexual purpose is served just like a train which leaves the station as soon as the signal is made. Joan Foster learns this truth at a heavy cost by placing herself in association with men who are eager to look at her from sexual angle only. All men whom she encounters are cheats who refuse to go beyond the sexual motive. The idea that a woman exists only for the purpose of sexual gratification and no other dimension worth-noting exists in her, is repulsive to Foster who feels that she is not at all a consumer-product for the purpose of sexual fulfillment.

Life on earth is like a detective story which runs with unknown events and unexpected consequences. The publication of

Joan Foster's novel, *Lady Oracle* and the subsequent T.V. interview drive Foster into contact with Fraser Buchanan who is a fake researcher and a pseudo Montreal poet. His devilish motive to make use of Foster as a consumer sex-product is brought out when he blackmails her, "The fact is, I know a good deal more about you than you think. I know things. I'm sure you would rather keep . . . private. Just between us two." (288) Buchanan's campaign is to probe into the sexual secrets embedded in the lives of women writers. His Black Notebook which unravels these private sexual lives is used as a weapon to blackmail women and achieve his sexual goals. Foster steals his note and escapes from his blackmail threats. Her novel is a plea for feminine literary space to reveal the sinister mind of man which runs after the body of woman. She lays bare through this novel how her love remains unrequited.

> I felt I'd never really loved anyone not Paul not Chuck the Royal Porcupine, not even Arthur. I'd polished them with my love and expected them to shine, brightly enough to return my own reflection enhanced and sparkling. (314-15)

The sad tragedy of Joan Foster is that she leaves everyone genuinely but no one equally responds to her. What stands in the way of this balanced transaction is the selfish attitude of man to use woman for his private sexual ends. Resisting the temptations of these men, Foster guards her individuality and refuses to be a consumer-product for the men she encounters.

So, Joan Foster sees in her own life and in the lives of others the phenomenon of sexual consumerism becoming identical with economic consumerism. In economic consumerism the focus is on the product whereas in sexual consumerism the focus is on the female who is reduced to the degenerate status of an object. In both processes, sexual and economic, the emphasis moves towards commoditizing and packaging. But sexual packaging which means using woman as a product for pleasure distresses Foster. She has seen seven men in her life: her father, aunt Lou's gambler husband, the Italian Cook Paul, Arthur, Chuck and Fraser Buchanan. None of these men is noble. The one principle common to all these men is exploitation of women as objects for sense enjoyment and sexual gratification. When she sees them running after the body of woman, she takes to writing where she takes cudgels against the sexual consumerism perpetuated by men. Atwood, in the ultimate analysis, attempts to reverse this phallocentric principle of consumerism and thereby celebrates woman who evolves into an artist in her novel, *Lady Oracle*.

Work Cited

Atwood, Margaret. *Lady Oracle*, New York: Avon Books, 1978.

Is Globalization an Attempt to Dehistoricize?: A Study of South Asian Canadian Novelists

D. PARAMESWARI
Madurai-Kamaraj University, Madurai

In Canada, since 1967 citizenship and immigration assess immigrants and visitors on standards which do not discriminate on the basis of race, national/ethnic origin, religion or sex. The Federal government's Immigration Act of 1976 which became law in 1978 and its amended version of 1993 reconfirmed the fundamental principle of non-discrimination and universality. This is Canada's move towards globalization.

The Canadians depended upon immigration from the very beginning. The colonists were immigrants. The French settled in Quebec, the British at Ontario. Each group multiplied and their descendants constitute the maximum percentage of Canadian population. After 1945, most of the immigrants came from countries devastated by World War II, particularly from Germany, Italy, Netherlands and Eastern Europe. By 1970s, over one quarter of the immigrant population in Canada was constituted by people from Asian countries like Hong Kong, India, Philippines, etc. These immigrants suffer discrimination, in spite of Canada's policy of non-discrimination, because one section in Canada's immigrant policy states that the policy should protect the Canadians also, by preventing the entry of potential criminals and terrorists. This clause is often used as a weapon to discriminate against anyone with whom the Canadians are displeased. The economic exploitation and deprivation of migrant labour force grow unchecked. The "Keep Canada White" cry also cannot be left unheard.

Then, to read the works of the South Asian Canadians as pictures of their paradisal existence in Canada is to efface history and posit that history never exists. To treat these non-natives i.e., the immigrants as Canadian citizens is to dehistoricize their suffering and attach an artificial sanctity to a life which they never live.

The present paper attempts to examine the predicament of the South Asian Canadians as seen in their representative works. All these South Asians are Immigrants by all possibilities. An immigrant shunting between two cultures, one of origin and the other of settlement, either (i) carves a new identity amalgamating the old and the new, and thus erases the obstructing margins of the polarized socio-cultural milieus, or, (ii) finds himself quite reluctant to bid farewell to his native soil. In the latter, both placed and displaced at once in the new land, he struggles hard to internalize his nostalgia. Past continues to persist, present also dominates; margins adamantly glare; the individual is tossed between two worlds, one distant, the other, immediate. The picture is that of a 'salad' bowl, to borrow a phrase used in the context of diasporic writing, where the individual components exist with distinct identities without any scope for merger.

The Indo-Caribbean writer in Canada is African, Canadian and Indian at once, for he is a synthesis of all these three. The poet Ramabai Espinet observes, "It is vital to remember that we are travellers moving with a lot of cultural baggage. We have not properly assessed this baggage" (Pillar 178). Ramabai and Madeline Coopsamy ponder over 'Migration,' 'Multiple Identities,' the after-effects of racial mixing, cultural hybridity and the need for developing a new, synthesized identity. In Ramabai's poem, "Hosary Night" (Nuclear 9) the persona, unlocking the "rusty iron lock memory," refers to the festive occasion of 'Hosary,' i.e. Muharram which commemorates the martyrdom of Prophet Mohamed. In Trinidad, the term no longer confines itself to one ethnic community; it has become a night festival, an occasion for celebration by a mixed population. The persona's reminiscence of the past is interwoven with the present reality of suffering, exploitation of ancestors at Trinidad and the struggle of the youngsters for survival at the new land, Canada.

These writers' exile sensibility first relates them to a blurring, questionable identity, then, subsequently paves way for a new heterogeneous one. Today, they have no one, distinct, homogeneous Indian/Caribbean, or South Asian identity. The poet Espinet explains, "We are people who emerged out of the South Asian Diaspora and are forming another Diaspora here." (Pillar 167) In the poem "Orthodoxies," Espinet cuts across edges, margins, boundaries and categories; she is cynical: "Are you a feminist? or simply a person? / . . . Black feminist / Caribbean feminist / Asian feminist . . . / Man-loving feminist / . . . cookist, womanist / super womanist / Not a feminist." (33) Construction of a multiple identity becomes an ongoing process and a strategy for survival among these immigrants.

The same phenomenon can be sighted in any other South Asians' settlement in Canada, a phenomenon that was commonly seen after the World Wars. By the 1970s, over one quarter of the new immigrants in Canada came from Asian countries such as Hong Kong, India and Philippines. Identity, dislocation, settlement, culture and home are the recurrent thematics in the writings of these immigrant writers, as the writers are either victims or beneficiaries of trans-national displacement.

While analyzing the problems of the Indian Diaspora in Canada, Uma Parameswaran writes, "Home is where our feet are, and we had better place our heart where the feet are." (1998: 39) The man who settles abroad as an immigrant finds a location, though he continues as an exile, suffering inevitable isolation. Then, which is his home?—the new land of which he has many dreams? Or, the one he has left behind?

The theme of home/homelessness is an age old issue pressing the mind of the indigenous population and the settlers, ever since man started travelling from place to place. One of the Trios in Indian English writing, Raja Rao once said, "I carry India with me wherever I go." Living away from Ireland, James Joyce wrote only about his native land, his "dear, dirty Dublin." Katherine Mansfield declared, "Wherever I live I write with New Zealand in my bones" (qtd. C.D. Narasimhaiah 9). The Poland-born Conrad, having left his country while it was struggling for freedom from the Russian rule, wrote volumes of essays and novels on every subject other than the slavery and the independence of his country, and subsequently suffered an acute sense of guilt life-long. For all immigrants, intense nostalgia is an inevitable outcome of their displacement. No move of the government towards globalization can solace them in their crisis.

The Palestinian Edward Said, born in Jerusalem but self-exiled to the U.S., emphasizes the schizophrenic inclination of the migrants caused by cultural dislocation and cross-fertilization. To Said, the migrant, in the course of his journey from homeland to an alien soil, first becomes 'tender,' then 'strong' and at last 'perfect.' He elaborates, "the person who finds his homeland sweet is still a tender beginner; he to whom every soil is as his native one is already strong, but he is perfect to whom the entire world is a foreign place. Survival is in fact about the-between-things (Said 407-8). The last phase is a very difficult one for an immigrant to attain.

The Indo-Canadian Stephen Gill's second novel *Immigrant* waxes eloquent over the trials and tribulations of an Indian immigrant in Canada. Reghu Nath's existence in Canada signals a shunting between a willful regression to India and a forced progression towards Canada, between the 'tender' and 'strong' phases. Gill creates a text and a context to cope with the politics of sharing and survival, the communication problems and socio-economic and political contradictions, ambiguities and racist and ethnic prejudices that cause disillusionment and distrust in an immigrant in every day life. (Singh 81) Many times Gill draws on his personal knowledge of the Asian's difficulty in adapting to a totally foreign political social clime. An interesting anecdote stands out. Gill's protagonist Reghu Nath, upon meeting an East Indian compatriot, warmly clasps hands and attempts to walk hand in hand. His newfound "friend, already tuned into North American mores, rejects Nath's gesture with a stern, 'This is not India.'" (20)

In an alien soil, he is restless and disturbed, with not a soul to help him. The rigid, demanding and prejudiced Professors at the University, the unfamiliar Canadian accent and register of the

English language, the confusing grading system, the adamant Canadian bureaucracy and the stubbornly haunting memories of India are his trouble-shooters. "Within a week Reghu found himself surrounded by many different problems. Financially, his position was not sound; educationally he did not know where he headed. Psychologically, he was yet not adjusted to his new environment." (15) At the University he finds himself open to the whims of his instructors and is compelled to accept what they demand from him. As for social life, it was almost non-existent. "The Professors and students used to come to class on time, then disperse mechanically soon after class was over." (15-16) He finds the Canadian women totally uncompromising and difficult. "He mustered all his courage to say politely 'I love you.' The girl glanced to one-side, then the other, before finishing her whisky in a gulp." (18) New words, unintelligible expressions and the Canadian slang take him unawares and baffle him totally.

Reghu Nath, ultimately, believes that since he chose to adopt Canada as home and forsake his native land, he can no longer turn back to his Asian nation where he would be taken as a failure both by his family and by the society. This is one typical example of the pathetic plight of the South Asian Canadians depicted by the Indian Gill.

Other Indian writers such as Rohinton Mistry or Shauna Singh Baldwin are also victims/ beneficiaries of displacement. Mistry emigrated to Canada in the 70s; his concerns are dislocation, relocation, home and world. Mistry always situates his stories in India, a land that is his no more; his stories are centred round in Parsi community in Bombay! Does it indicate a belated rediscovery of his roots? Is it because identity is more than a case of geographical location? In the last short story in *Tales from Firozsha Baag*, the father focuses on the need for assimilation of an immigrant. In "Squatter," another short story, uncle Nariman tells the tale of Sarosh that Sarosh had promised to return home if he does not become completely Canadian in ten years. Ten years pass by and Sarosh has to at last return home. Shauna Singh Baldwin's short story, "Montreal 1962" spins round a couple who have emigrated to Canada. The man has been warned that he must stop wearing his turban if he wants to keep his job. Holding on to the practice of wearing the turban signifies resistance to the homogenizing claims of the adopted space, i.e., Canada. The Indian persists in resisting.

While Mistry thus casts a long lingering look at his dear native soil, the Sri Lanka born Michael Ondaatje, hailing from a family of mixed Dutch, Singhalese and Tamil ancestry, reveals traces of his desire for his ancestral home on one hand and a tendency towards assimilation on the other, with his involvement in the local issues of the adopted country in his *The English Patient* and *In the Skin of a Lion*. In his autobiography, *Running in the Family*, Ondaatje talks of how when he visited Sri Lanka twenty five years after he left it he engaged himself in recollecting pieces of experience, family history, local legends and family scandals. The book is a feat of memory reflecting the complex impulses of a son of the soil.

Similarly, Cyril Dabydeen, the Indian-Guyanese-Canadian, in his essay "India in Me" proclaims that he will continue to write (about) India while longing for a real home or place (Qtd. Begum 138); Canada, on the other hand, has fed him, has "nourished, brought to fruition his professional skill as a narrator." (Begum 65) Bicultural pulls loom large in Dabydeen's writings. Dabydeen finds Diaspora a reiterative, obsessive and oppressive experience; the movement of his ancestors from India to Guyana was re-enacted in his own migration from Guyana to Canada. Movement, then, is one long continuum. His poem "Encounter" in the collection, *Goatsong*, envelops the false promise of a new land, leading to "Separation" (the title of another poem), the inevitable corollary of movement.

"Relations," a short story of Dabydeen in the collection *Jogging in Havana* spins round the fat Goldie and her wanderer-communist husband. The story embodies the Caribbeans' views about India and its abiding culture. Goldie's mother expects her daughter to behave "like an Indian movie star, Vijayantimala or Nargis." The admiration of these Indians for their native soil i.e., India, is so deep-rooted that they "would watch Indian movies at the local cinema . . . and for days after, every one talked about the episode . . . And the stars became household names." They spent their time "fantasizing about places like Bombay and Delhi, so far away from Guyana, yet close." (15)

Arun Mukherjee celebrates the writings of Dabydeen in contrast to those of Ondaatje on the ground that the latter obscures the social and political realities by taking a universalistic stance whereas the nourishing strength of Dabydeen's works emanates from their concrete political context. The governing motifs of Dabydeen's collection, *Jogging in Havana*, are a longing to return to the native culture, alongside an acute struggle for recognition in the new.

In the short story "Jogging in Havana," Deidre, the New-Yorker in Canada, walking down the memory-lane, often mutters about her childhood when she could skate in Madison Square Garden. Then, Slokan Charles, the Cuba-born intellectual, now an academic at Illinois State University, after his countless visits to his motherland in the past years, affirms: "I wish to go back to Guyana, after Havana; I should be in touch with my roots." (51) The guide at the dining table of the conference-site, the man who has never travelled beyond Cuba, when questioned, snaps, "there are many Cubans coming back to our island because life in Miami, in America failed them." "It was a dog-eating dog society, and the dope, gambling, unemployment, alienation . . . it was too much for them." (56) Animated by "history and heritage," this guide declines to suffer the trauma of uprootedness.

In another short-story titled "Places," parents are eager to send the little Anil to Canada with his uncle. Anil, not at all tempted by the alleged prospectus of the distant green land, exhibits his defiance. "Do you want to go back with me to Canada? No, he replied." (12) As the story concludes, the boy who all the while reluctantly refined his manners and gestures in order to join his sophisticated uncle at Canada, bursts out in laughter and excitement in the crowd of his friends. The situation connotes the wayward and repentant son's homecoming and his fraternity embracing him with warmth and love.

In "The Pooja Man," the crippling influence of the new soil is paramount. The central motif of "The Pooja Man" pertaining to the expatriate who, due to the expiry of his visa, runs from pillar to post in order to escape from the immigration officials, sets Guyana and Canada in contrast, one affluent, the other, "virtually did not have anything, the inhabitants were virtually starving." (35) The Canadian government discourages the Guans from seeking refuge in Canada on false excuses and mercilessly deports the illegals as soon as they are traced. The mother in this story wants her sons to run away from Guyana since she cannot bear her children perishing for want of food and sustenance for their physical and spiritual well-being.

Fleeing, running away or jogging appear to be a binding motif in Cyril Dabydeen. At the end of the story "Jogging in Havana," Dr. Slokan Charles's jogging in Havana symbolizes a fond desire to return to the native country, a fascination for its land and sea; in "The Pooja man" the narrator visualizes his expatriate brother "running away, dragging his wife with him" (44), escaping the immigration officials. In all these contexts, movement, i.e., Slokan's jogging and the expatriate's "running," capture the immigrant's escape from an agonizing present, along with their lingering memories of an idyllic past. The past/the homeland which the immigrant willingly or reluctantly left and the present, the newfound land which offers him succour vie with each other in order to take the lead and hence, the immigrant's running.

All these South Asian Canadians, thus, mostly, subsume under their native identity. In their life and writings, margins glare and intrude. Canada as a nation may celebrate multiculturalism and globalization. It aims at integrating different ethnic groups and immigrants. However, these settlers, though outwardly getting integrated in Canada's social mosaic, preserve their own native cultural identity and heritage. Canadian policy may attempt to dehistoricize by undercutting history and etymology, but history cannot be effaced. There are adamant ghettoes that nullify nation's efforts to merge them all under one umbrella. These ghettoes will exist forever, alongside Canada's policy of globalization.

Works Cited

Bhabha, Homi. *Nations and Narrations*. London: Routledge, 1990.

Begum, Jameela. *Writers of the Indian Diaspora: Cyril Dabydeen*. New Delhi: Rawat, 2000.

Dabydeen, Cyril. *Jogging in Havana*. Ontario: Mosaic Press, 1992.

_____, "India in Me: Reflections," *Writers of the Indian Diaspora: Cyril Dabydeen*. Jameela Begum (New Delhi: Rawat, 2000).

Espinet, Ramabai, *Nuclear Seasons*. Toronto: Sister Vision, 1991.

_____, Interview with Birbalsingh in *From Pillar to Post*. Toronto: TSAR, 1997.

Gill, Stephen. *Immigrant*. Ontario: Vesta, 1982.

Mukherjee, Arun P. "The Poetry of Michael Ondaatje and Cyril Dabydeen: Two Responses to Otherness." *Journal of Commonwealth Literature*, 20:1 (1985): 49-67.

Narasimhaiah, C.D. *Essays in Commonwealth Literature: Heirloom of Multiple Heritage*. Delhi: San Park Press, 1995.

Parameswaran, Uma. "Home is Where Your Feet are, and May Your Heart be There Too," *Writers of Indian Diaspora: Theory and Practice*, ed. Jasbir Jain. New Delhi: Rawat, 1998.

Phillips, Bluebell S. "Two Novels of Gill," *Glimpses: A Selection of Published Articles about Stephen Gill and His Books* (Ontario: Vesta, 1999).

Said, Edward. *Culture and Imperialism*. London. Vintage, 1994.

_____, *The Politics of Dispossession*, London: Vintage, 1995.

Singh, R.K. "Cross Cultural Communications," *Language Forum*, Vol. XXIV, No. 1-2, Jan.-Dec. 1998.

Interpretation of Gender in Postcolonial Literary Text: Case of a Malaysian writer

Jariah Mohd. Jan
University of Malaya, Kuala Lumpur

Abstract

Most written products that are considered creative, particularly in terms of plots, contexts and characters are created based on the writers' observations on the reality of their surroundings. It has been observed that members of most cultures and societies have certain perceptions or stereotype views of the behaviour of men and women regarding styles in dressing, activities, career and social roles in society. Writers rely on these usually stereotyped and generalized observations and portray these traits in their writing especially in their characters in order to make their written products believable, real and effective.

This study sets out to examine the effect of gender differences as depicted in a novel, Salina, *written by a Malaysian. The contention of this paper is: 1) to analyse the stereotyped characteristics of male and female speech styles as portrayed by the non-native writer in the Malaysian novel; 2) to examine whether the western perceptions of gender differences in speech styles exist in the Malaysian literature.*

The linguistic features that are used for basis of analysis include superpolite forms, and hedges. The analysis is focused on the use of these features by the characters in the novel. The findings of the study suggest that there are gender differences in the use of these features and that the western perceptions of the gendered speech styles are not reflected in the Malaysian society.

There have been numerous hypotheses formed on the relationship between people's general expectations and beliefs about men and women and the behaviour of members of these groups (Worrell; Taylor and Hall). In most societies, men and women see themselves as conforming to the typical behaviour of their sex group. This might involve characteristics of gender-biased costumes, activities, areas of expertise and social roles in society as well as differences in ways of communicating.

Our constructs of masculinity and femininity influence our reactions to men and women. The moment we have categorized someone as a male or female, 'our gender constructs come into play, providing us with judgmental standards against which to compare a person in forming impression about their masculinity and femininity' (Smith, 28). Thus, in a particular society, men and women conform to the accepted and desired characteristics, as society's expectations and perceptions shape their behaviour in that society.

Various researchers have pointed out that there are differences in ways of communicating between male and female (Lakoff, 1975; Spender; Coates, 1986; Tannen, 1991; Jariah Mohd. Jan). However, most empirically based studies of differences between male and female speech styles have been dealt with in the naturally occurring or 'real life' conversations in the public sphere (Fishman, 1983; Coates, 1986; Jariah Mohd. Jan, 1999). There has been very little evidence of studies on gender conversational styles in writing particularly in literary texts such as in novels, short stories, plays or screenplays. This study intends to examine this area of male and female conversational styles with a focus on speech crafted by a Malaysian author in literary text.

Most written products that are considered creative, particularly in terms of plots, contexts and characters are created based on the writers' observations on the reality of their surroundings. It has been observed that members of most cultures and societies have certain perceptions or stereotype views of the behaviour of men and women regarding styles in dressing, activities, career and social roles in society. Writers rely on these usually stereotyped and generalized observations and portray these traits in their writing especially in their characters in order to make their written products believable and effective. For instance, the stereotype view of gender characteristics in the society is portrayed by the differences in ways of communicating between men and women. As such, the speech styles that are associated with either male or female are often crafted by writers in their stories to make their fictitious characters seems real and acceptable to the readers.

This paper attempts to examine the effect of gender differences as depicted in a selected novel written by a Malaysian literary writer. The contention of this paper is: 1) to analyse the stereotyped characteristics of male and female speech styles as portrayed by the non-native writer in the Malaysian novel; 2) to examine whether the western perceptions of gender differences in speech styles exist in the Malaysian literature.

In any society, men and women vary in the degree to which they see themselves as conforming to gendered typical norms of personality and behaviour. The cultural norms that are regulated in a society according to the social desire of that society itself is referred to as behavioural construct. These norms may include social roles in society, occupation, and language use.

Frank and Ashen note that society plays an important part in the social function of the language; that language differences are due in part to our social expectations. For instance, since most of behavioural constructs in terms of cultural norms are regulated in accordance with the values of men, we tend to respond to boys and girls differently. Our level of acceptance of their behaviour may differ. For example, it is generally accepted for boys and men to be dominant, aggressive, independent and objective. Girls and women, on the other hand, are more likely to be accepted as submissive, dependent, passive and subjective. As such, women are expected to 'act as a lady' and 'respect those around you' reflects the role of inferior status, that is women, being expected to respect their superior who are men. These behavioural constructs have empowered men while women are considered as one-step below men or rather a secondary status in the society. This encoding behaviour of men and women in the society has significant ramifications on the way they communicate and socialize in inter-gender interactions.

Inevitably, our social expectations and experiences may be a contributing factor to the language differences or differing linguistic styles between men and women at any time and in any situation.

There have been numerous studies that appear to support the idea of stylistic gender differences in conversation. Lakoff's observations (1975 and 1977) of women's language are considered as one of the earliest made regarding the differences in speech styles between men and women which arise based on the consequences of social inequalities between sexes.

According to Robin Lakoff, the style of language which was typically used by women and thus denied them 'the means to express [themselves] strongly,' and instead make them sound 'trivial' and 'uncertain' were as follows:

i The use of words connected with women's culture (colour terms, sewing terms) which are not in men's vocabulary, or are used disparagingly by men.

ii So-called "empty" adjectives, such as "divine". and "charming."

iii Tag questions and rising intonation used with grammatically declarative utterances.

iv The use of hedges to avoid being too assertive or direct.

v The use of "so" as an intensifier, as in "I like him so much."

vi Hypercorrect forms in pronunciation and grammar.

vii Being "superpolite."

viii Not telling jokes.

ix Speaking in *italics* (which presumably refers to women's stress patterns). (Lakoff, 1975:53-56)

Lakoff was working on the principle that women's speech patterns are *worse* than men's, in that they confirm women's subordinate social status and prevent them from being treated as equals.

In 1977, Lakoff further characterizes her basic assumptions of women's speech styles under three main categories, namely Lexical traits, Phonological traits and Syntactic-Pragmatic Traits.

A Summary of the Characteristics of Women's Speech Styles (Lakoff, 1977)

No.	Female Speech Styles	Speech Characteristics
1.	Lexical Traits	• Special lexicon • Imprecise intensifiers • super polite forms
2.	Phonological Traits	• hypercorrect grammar • clear & precise pronunciation
3.	Syntactic-Pragmatic Traits	• epistemic modality and hedges • tag questions • direct quotations

This study will only focus on two linguistic features proposed by Lakoff (1977) for basis of analysis which include super polite forms, and hedges.

Holmes refers to 'politeness' as an expression of concern for the feelings of others and that people may express concern for others' feelings in many ways, both linguistic and non-linguistic. Being polite means expressing respect towards the person you are talking to and avoiding offending them. In other words, politeness may take the form of an expression of good-will or camaraderie, establishing good rapport, as well as the more familiar non-intrusive behaviour which is labelled 'polite' in everyday usage. Correctly identifying what is perceived as polite behaviour in a culture involves understanding the society's values.

Malaysians observe a politeness system that embodies specific codes of verbal and non-verbal behaviour in their interactions with others (Jamaliah Mohd. Ali, 1995b: 65). They are generally receptive to those who display good manners in face-to-face interaction. In the Malay community, it is expected of the Malays to be polite or demonstrate finesse in behaviour whenever they interact with others. This is evident especially in interaction that involves persons of a certain institutional or societal rank. Such behaviour indicates proper upbringing. The notion of relational distance, respect for elders, hierarchical position as well as status and authority are very much rooted in the Malay value system (Jariah Mohd. Jan, 206).

Some aspects of behaviour that Malaysians consider may demonstrate finesse are as follows (Asmah Haji Omar, 23-24):

- Not being forthright or assertive or aggressive;
- Not being blunt or direct in expressing one's views;
- Not causing interpersonal conflict or avoiding 'loss of face.'

When someone is being polite, there are many possible features of their use of the language that are being referred to. Polite people tend to phrase their utterances considerately, respond encouragingly and positively to others' talk, and express appreciation generously. They avoid confrontation, public displays, being too forceful or direct because these are all examples of behaviour which are regarded as impolite, coarse, rude, and may even suggest ill-breeding (Jamaliah Mohd. Ali, 1991).

Lakoff (1975) observes that in women's speech, there is also a more frequent expressions of emotions such as love, endearment, and grief, avoidance of angry and hostile expressions. In doing so, women tend to use super polite forms and euphemistic forms such as 'would you mind. . .,' 'I'd aprreciate it if. . .' and ' . . . if you don't mind.'

Jamaliah Mohd. Ali (1995b: 75) stipulates that the norms of society require that we abide by social rules in our daily interactions. As such, 'face' is one of the mechanisms at the level of social interaction to maintain not only the stability of the interactants but that of the interaction as well.

In Malaysia, the concept of face-saving means saving another person, or oneself, from embarrassment. In other words, the speaker tries not to put the listener or himself in a position in which he or she might be embarrassed. The 'face' that a person maintains becomes important especially when it is subjected to risk and assumes significance particularly when events are being interpreted and evaluated. Therefore, it must be constantly attended to in interaction.

Ostman (4) explains that the 'face-saving' aspect of verbal and (non-verbal) behaviour is characterised by an egocentric, direct and efficient expression of wants and needs whilst the politeness aspect, works at suppressing such potential egocentricity and prevents it from occurring overtly in behaviour.

In general, people try to build up each other's 'positive face' (the positive image that people have and want to be appreciated and approved by others) and avoid posing threats to the 'negative face' (where one's actions should not be impeded by others) in co-operative interaction.

Behaviour which avoids imposing on others or avoids 'threatening their face' is described as evidence of negative politeness, while sociable behaviour expressing warmth towards an addressee is positive politeness behaviour (Brown and Levinson). According to this approach, any utterance which could be interpreted as making a demand or intruding on another person's autonomy can be regarded as a potential face-threatening act (henceforth FTA). Polite people avoid obvious FTAs, such as insults and orders. They usually attempt to reduce the threat of unavoidable FTAs such as requests or warnings by softening them, or expressing them indirectly; and they use positively polite utterances such as greetings and compliments where possible.

The mutual relationship between the participants in an interaction is very significant in deciding the degree of face threat. For instance, something that is fairly minimally face-threatening in private encounters, such as, a friendly talk, becomes highly face-threatening in public encounters. Competent conversation participants often look for ways that can minimise the threat to face in one way or another. This of course requires an ability to reach each other's signals and to accommodate each other's wants. Furthermore, preserving each other's face in social interactions is very important in maintaining harmony and stability. Failure to do so may result in undesirable communicative consequences. As such, this phenomenon at times imposes further constraints on the conversational behaviour of the participants.

Epistemic modality refers to the linguistic forms which speakers use to express their degree of commitment to the truth of a proposition. The forms that realise speakers' commitment are typically modal auxiliary verbs such as 'should,' 'would,' 'could,' ' may' and 'might.' Other linguistic forms that fulfil the same function are items such as 'perhaps,' 'really,' and also hedges such as 'sort of,' 'I think' and 'kind of.'

According to Lakoff (1975: 53), hedges are "words that convey the sense that the speaker is uncertain about what he or she is saying or cannot vouch for the accuracy of the statement." The speaker only uses hedges as one of the strategies to express his or her personal attitude or comment to the utterance made in the conversation. Coates defines it by the function of items, rather than their grammatical category. According to Coates (1989: 113): "Epistemic modal forms are defined semantically as those linguistic forms which are used to indicate the speaker's confidence or lack of confidence in the truth of the proposition expressed in the utterance. If someone says, *Perhaps she missed the train*, the use of the word *perhaps* indicates the lack of confidence in the proposition 'she missed the train.' Lexical items such as *perhaps, I think, sort of, probably*, as well as certain prosodic and paralinguistic features, are used in English to express epistemic modality."

Coates (*Ibid.*: 113-14) also extends the functions usually associated with epistemic modal forms: "Such forms, however, are used by speakers not just to indicate their lack of commitment to the truth of propositions, but also to hedge assertions in order to protect both their own and addressees' face."

She contends that women, especially in single-sex groups, exploit these forms more than men and they use them to mitigate the force of an utterance in order to respect the addressees' face needs (*Ibid.*). In order to illustrate this point, Coates (*Ibid.*) cites the following example: "[speaker describes an old friend she's recently bumped into] she looks very *sort of* um(-) *kind of* matronly I *really*." She claims that the italicised forms in the example given above "hedge the assertion she looks matronly not because the speaker doubts its truth but because she does not want to offend her addressees by assuming their agreement (describing a friend in unflattering terms is controversial)" (*Ibid.*).

The suggestion here is that the instances of epistemic modal forms above have one function of protecting the face of the speaker's addressees, by permitting their dissent from the truth content of her proposition. However, Coates emphasises that the polypragmatic nature of forms also protects the speaker's face. In this instance, the speaker in the example can retreat from the proposition expressed if it turns out to be unacceptable. She concludes that "Presumably such topics do not trigger the use of epistemic modal forms because they are not so face-threatening" (*Ibid.*). In addition, hedges also function as politeness strategies often used by women in their speech (*Ibid*, 1986).

A Malaysian novel, *Salina*, by A. Samad Said who is a renowned Malaysian literary writer was selected for this study. For the purpose of analysis, a translated version of *Salina* by Hawa Abdullah was used. Unlike many other translated versions, this is close to the original Malay version. The originality of the spoken or colloquial Malay language is very well translated and maintained.

Salina is regarded as the line of demarcation which separates the early writers from the present ones (Hanna Sheikh Mokhtar). The style used by the author differs from other writers in that it is told by the means of dialogues or conversations among the characters, which reflect the social life and mannerisms as expected by the society they dwell in.

The story depicts the struggles confronted by women in order to survive in the male-dominated world. Thus, women in *Salina* represent a new breed of women who were modernised by colonial rule and were toughened by Japanese occupation.

Five excerpts from *Salina* that featured the conversations of male and female characters portrayed by the writer were selected at random. The excerpts were randomly selected to avoid inclination towards the existence of the features of the speech styles if they were studied and analyzed beforehand.

In analyzing the male and female speech styles in the selected excerpts, the speech styles portrayed by the characters were identified based on the linguistic features stipulated by Lakoff (1975) namely, super polite forms and hedges. Examples were extracted and quoted from the excerpts as evidence of the use of the linguistic features by the characters (as written by the writer).

The aspects of the phonological traits of the discourse that include intonation and voice pitch were not included as there would be no indication of such in the written text. The following table summarizes the speech characteristics that were examined in the study:

Examples of Linguistic Features Examined in *Salina*

No.	Female Speech Styles	Speech Characteristics	Examples
1.	Lexical Traits	Super polite forms Expletives • Strong expletives • Weak expletives	• *Would you mind . . .* • *Could you please . . .* • *Damn, I'll be damn, Shit, Hell* • *My goodness . .* • *Oh, dear ,. . .*
2.	Syntactic-Pragmatic Traits	Epistemic modality and hedges • Modal auxiliary • Modal adverbs • Qualifying adjectives • Egocentric sequences	• *May, might, could* • *Perhaps, possibly, may be* • *So, very,* • *I believe, I think, I guess*

In general, the data analyses show that most of the characters in *Salina* are quite polite to each. It is difficult to measure linguistic politeness as claimed by Holmes (110) because "not only is there an infinite variety of ways of expressing linguistic politeness, it is also the case that the same linguistic devices can express different meanings in different contexts. There is nothing intrinsically polite about any linguistic form."

Although the politeness in the characters' speech is not illustrated evidently in terms of the use of special words, or phrase, both the men's and women's speech styles conform to Holmes' descriptions of politeness; that "polite people tend to phrase their utterances considerately, respond encouragingly and positively to others' talk, pay compliments, and express appreciation generously" (24-25). This is a typical feature of the Malaysian culture that "when talking, we need to moderate our voice, and not talk in a way that hurt other's feeling" (Shasel). Except for two instances of the use of *please*, there is no other evidence of the use of other polite forms in speech among the female characters.

- *Idah, Please sit down . . .* p 283
- *Please light it, my hands are wet.* p 212

There is some evidence of the use of expletives among male characters in *Salina*. The findings show that there is only one instance of strong expletive attributing to male style while the weak forms are those used by the male characters and that are attributed to the female style.

Strong and Weak Expletives used by Male Characters in *Salina*

Strong Expletives	Weak Expletives
That wretched tramp! He doesn't know his place . . . p. 76	*If you become dead wood in the house, goodness, the tramp will take advantage. . .* p. 321 *My! Oh my!* P. 324 *Lo and behold after that, the clerk disappears for months.* P. 325 *Very well! You say it is difficult . . .* p. 79

The underlined words are uttered by Abdul Fakar, one of the male characters in *Salina*. He is portrayed as a womanizer and because he flirts with women, the language he uses reflects his intentions. Almost always he speaks in the manner that women prefer. For example, he would speak gently and appears to understand women very well.

The linguistic features used by Abdul Fakar indicate that his speech lacks male characteristics. As such, except for the strong expletive mentioned earlier, all the other expletives used are weak and considered having feminine style.

Other expletives found in the excerpts are:

- *Oh dear, you shouldn't have troubled yourself, sis. . .* p. 47
- *Oh! Such a pity!* p. 198
- *Praise be to God.* p. 198

Another male character in *Salina* who uses these weak forms of expletives is Hilmi. He is portrayed as an educated person, as well as polite and respectful to others. His religious background and upbringing cause him to watch his language when speaking to others. Thus, his use of expletives is not typical of male's speech style.

It appears that the female characters use more weak forms of expletives compared to the male characters in *Salina*. They also use forms of endearment such as *dear* and *my sweet* as shown in the following table.

The Use of Polite Forms and Expletives in *Salina*

Female Speech Styles	Male Speech Styles
Dear me! Exercising so early in the morning? p. 36 *Goodness! What a hope!* p. 39 *How long is it since he passed away?* p. 45	*Dear me! If it is as you say, the landlord's simply squeezing money from us.* p. 40 *Oh dear you shouldn't have troubled yourself, sis . . .* p. 47 *Oh dear! Why swear?* p. 86 *Goodness! Tonight, I'll give you a treat.* p. 89

Goodness, it's been going on for so long, how could you not know? p. 75 *Dear, why do you like to go to Razman's house*? p. 119 *Do you want me to apply some ointment to your eyes, dear?* p. 122 *Goodness! Now you say: Praise be to God.* p. 198 *I am fond of you, my sweet*. p. 210 *Idah, Please sit down . . .* p. 283 *Please light it, my hands are wet*. p. 212	*Good Gracious! You embarrass me, of course I have the money.* p. 90 *Dear me, what a shame!* p. 247 *Oh my sweet. You are clever to talk, aren't you?* p. 288 *...,How clever you are, my sweet.* p. 289 *Oh dear, you shouldn't have troubled yourself, sis . . .* p. 47 *Oh! Such a pity!* p. 198 *Praise be to God*. p. 198 *If you become dead wood in the house, goodness, the tramp will take advantage. . .* p. 321 *My! Oh my!* p. 324 *Lo and behold after that, the clerk disappears for months.* p. 325 *Very well! You say it is difficult . . .* p. 79

There are seven types of hedges used by both male and female characters in *Salina*. The use of this feature is tabulated below. Contrary to the assumptions that hedges are exclusively a female speech style, there is considerable evidence of the use of this feature in male speech.

Gender and Distribution of Hedges in *Salina*

No.	Types of Hedges	Male	Female	Total
A	**Modal Adverbs**			
1.	Really	15	8	23
2.	Perhaps	9	5	14
3.	Surely	7	6	13
	Total	31	19	50

B	**Modal Auxiliary**			
1.	Would	15	5	20
2.	Should	6	2	8
3.	Could	3	2	5
4.	Must	10	2	12
	Total	34	11	45
C	**Adjectives**			
1.	Too	6	1	7
2.	So	23	8	31
	Total	29	9	38
D	**Egocentric**			
1.	I know	16	6	22
2.	I do / I don't	24	15	39
3.	I think	8	1	9
4.	I hope	4	0	4
5.	I want	6	0	6
6.	I feel	2	0	2
	Total	60	22	82
E	**Fillers**			
1.	Well	13	6	19
2.	of course	8	5	13
3.	you know	11	6	17
	Total	32	17	49
	Total (A+B+C+D+E)	186	78	264

The above data shows that in contrast with the expectations based on the perceptions of the gender speech styles, the male characters have been portrayed to use more hedges compared to the female characters. This finding on the use of hedges, contradicts the claim made by Lakoff (1975) and other researchers

(Coates; Githens; Jariah Mohd. Jan) that women use these features more than men do.

As can be seen above, the male characters in *Salina* use more hedges, especially the egocentric types such as *I do/I don't* and *I know*, compared to the female characters. The assertive behaviour of the male characters is reflected in their use of hedges (60 items). On the other hand, the female characters appear to be less assertive and seldom relate their needs and true feelings about matters that are of importance to them.

The findings of the study suggest that there are gender differences in the use of these features. The speech styles portrayed in *Salina* do exhibit the linguistic features of male and female. However, unlike the previous claims (Lakoff, 1975; Tannen, 1990; Githens; Jariah Mohd. Jan), these stylistic features seem not to be exclusively used by one gender only. Both male and female characters in the novel are portrayed as using them. Although the speech characteristics in this study have been claimed as associated with female speech style, the results of this study show that it is the particular requirement of the conversations that motivate the use by either a male or a female. It is suggested that the occurrence of the styles portrayed in the male and female speech is not determined or influenced by gender of an individual speaker but by the context itself.

In most studies, the claims of gendered speech styles have been made based on the western perceptions. In *Salina*, however, both men and women characters have been pictured to have used similar linguistic features in their conversations. The characters are also portrayed to be sensitive to the behaviour of their conversational partners and thus alter their speech accordingly.

The western perceptions of the gendered speech styles are not reflected in the Malaysian literature. Thus, it is suggested that the generalizations made in the west on the speech styles of male and female cannot be generalized in the speech styles of male and female in other contexts or societies. It seems reasonable to conclude that writers, regardless of their culture and societal background appear to perceive or conceptualize male and female speech as a collaborative social activity rather than being restricted in personal traits. As such, when they write the speech for their characters in a novel, they take into account aspects such as the role and status of the characters in the society and the context of the conversation rather than the gender of the interlocutors.

Perhaps it would be best to conclude that the perception of the different speech styles between men and women lies in our own belief and perception. To a certain extent, people tend to exaggerate perceived differences in the verbal styles of men and women because we live in an environment that stresses differences rather than similarities.

Works Cited

A. Samad Said. 1991. *Salina*, trans. Hawa Abdullah. Kuala Lumpur: Dewan Bahasa dan Pustaka.

Asmah Haji Omar. 1992. *The Linguistic Scenery in Malaysia.* Kuala Lumpur: Dewan Bahasa dan Pustaka.

Brown, P. and S. Levinson. 1987. "Universals in Language Usage: Politeness Phenomena," E.N. Goody, ed., *Questions and Politeness: Strategies in Social Interaction.* Cambridge: Cambridge University Press, 58-289.

Coates, J. 1986. *Women, Men and Language: A Sociolinguistic Account of Gender Differences in Language.* Second Edition. London: Longman.

_____. 1989. "Gossip Revisited: Language in All-Female Groups." In J. Coates and D. Cameron, ed., *Women in Their Speech Communities.* London: Longman.

Fishman, P. 1983. "Interaction: The Work Women Do." In B. Thorne, C. Kramarae and N. Henley, ed., *Language, Gender and Society*, Cambridge: Newbury House Publishers, 89-101.

Frank, F. and F. Ashen. 1983. *Language and the Sexes.* University of New York Press, Albany.

Githens, S. 1991. Men, Women in Conversation: An Analysis of Gender Styles in Language. [On-line] Available: http//www.georgetown.edu.bassr/githens/otto1922.htm

Hanna Sheikh Mokhtar. 1993. "The Portrayal of Women in A Samad Said's *Salina.*" Unpublished Thesis, UPM, Serdang, Selangor.

Holmes, J. 1995. *Women, Men and Politeness.* London: Longman.

Jamaliah Mohd. Ali. 1991. *The Academic Seminar as an Arena for Cognitive Conflict and Conflict Resolution: A Malaysian Context.* Working Paper No. 9. Project on Culturally Conditioned Models of Conflict Resolution. Gothenburg, Sweden: Centre for East and South East Asian Studies, University of Gothenburg, Sweden.

_____. 1995a. The Pragmatics of Cross-Cultural Communication in a Malaysian Context. In Zainab Abdul Majid and Loga Mahesan Baskaran, ed., *Rules of Speaking: Verbal Interaction at Play.* Pelanduk Publications, 112-24.

_____. 1995b. *Malaysian Student Seminar: A Study of Pragmatic Features in Verbal Interaction.* Unpublished Ph.D. Thesis, University of Malaya, Kuala Lumpur.

Jariah Mohd. Jan. 1999. *Malaysian Talk Shows: A Study of Power and Solidarity in Inter-Gender Verbal Interaction.* Unpublished Ph.D. Thesis, University of Malaya, Kuala Lumpur, Malaysia.

Lakoff, R. 1975. *Language and Women's Place.* Harper and Row, New York.

_____. 1977. *Language and Women's Place.* New York: Harper and Row.

Ostman, J. 1981. *You Know. A Discourse Functional Approach.* Amsterdam: John Benjamins.

Shasel, P. 1997. Restore Malay/Islamic Courtliness. [Online] Available: http://www.ioi.ie/~/afifi/BICNews/shasel/shasel3.htm

Smith, P. 1985. *Language, the Sexes and Society.* Cornwall: Basil Blackwell.

Spender, J. and R. Helmreich. 1975. *Masculinity and Femininity: Their Psychological Dimensions, Correlates and Antecedents.* Austin, Texas: University of Texas Press.

Tannen, D. 1990. "Gender Differences in Topical Coherence: Creating Involvement in Best Friend's Talk." In B. Dorval ed., *Conversational Organisation and its Development.* Norwood, New Jersey: Ablex.

_____. 1991. *You Just Don't Understand: Women and Men in Conversation.* London: Virago.

Taylor, M. and J. Hall. 1982. "Psychological Androgyny: Theories, Methods and Conclusions." *Psychological Bulletin*, 92 (2), 347-66.

Worrel, J. 1978. "Sex Roles and Psychological Well-Being: Perspectives on Methodology." *Journal of Consulting and Clinical Psychology*, 46 (4), 777-91.

Generational Differences in Diasporic Writings: Jhumpa Lahiri's *The Namesake*

SUNITA AGARWAL
Rajasthan University, Jaipur

Jumpa Lahiri's Pulitzer Prize winning collection of short sto ries *Interpreter of Maladies; Stories of Bengal and Boston and Beyond* focuses on the lives of Indians in exile. She very subtly brings out the conflict of these immigrants between the traditions they have inherited and the day-to-day life they encounter. In her second work *The Namesake*, a fiction, she again deals with the theme of identity crisis and the problem of assimilation and adaptation in another country. The novel is a story of two generations--Ashoke and Ashima on the one hand and their children Gogol and Sonia on the other, and their life period of thirty years. The novel begins in the year 1968, the birth year of Gogol and stretches to the year 2000, depicting the different attitudes, outlooks and directionality of two generations in dealing with the problems in a foreign country. They face different problems as the meaning of culture differs for both the generations, the first being directly related to his/her homeland and second generation forming an image of culture based on the information transmitted by the first generation. The present paper proposes to deal with these generational differences in diasporic culture with reference to the novel *The Namesake*.

The novel opens in a nostalgic mood, Ashima, the wife of Ashoke, the protagonist, in her advanced stage of pregnancy, is eating puffed rice with lots of spices and lemon, an Indian concoction sold in Calcutta's sidewalk for pennies, the taste being not the same brings her the memories of her homeland. Ashoke, an MIT engineer, has migrated to Boston to obliterate the memories of a train accident he met with; thus it is a self-imposed migration. In spite of his well-settled life there, his return to India to marry a Bengali girl asserts his desire to retain his separate identity and solidarity to homeland. Ashima, for all her efforts to settle in a new way of life, felt homesick in that alien country. She felt uprooted and lived in a world of nostalgia. She spent hours in the apartment napping and sulking, rereading her parents' letters and the same five Bengali novels time and again. For Ashima, "Being a foreigner is a sort of lifelong pregnancy" a perpetual wait, a constant burden, a continuous feeling out of sort. Like pregnancy, being a foreigner, Ashima believed is something that elicits "the same curiosity from strangers, the same combination of pity and respect." (50) The dichotomy between public and private sphere is almost tormenting to these women immigrants who have to suffer double dependence. It becomes difficult for them to cope with multiple stresses of the two different cultures. They have to reconstruct their gender identity and locate themselves in the host culture.

Ashima gave birth to a child in a country where she is related to no one, where she knows little, where life seems so tentative and spare. The boy was named Gogol, after the name of the Russian writer Nikolai Gogol who is associated with the memories of the train accident. In fact Ashoke owed his second birth to him. At the time of the train accident, he was reading the story "The Overcoat" by Gogol and it was with the fluttering of its page that the attention of the rescuing party was drawn to Ashoke and he was saved. As Gogol grew, Ashoke and Ashima's circle of Bengali acquaintances also increased. The very fact that all belong to one country is reason enough for them to relate and form their own ethnic group and community. "They all come from Calcutta, and for this reason alone they are all friends. Most of them live within walking distance of one another in Cambridge." (38) This diasporic community preserves their separate identity by observing their tradition. As Safran (1991) has observed, it is a general characteristic of diasporic that "they continue to relate, personally or vicariously to the homeland in one way or other and their ethno-communal consciousness and solidarity are importantly defined by the existence of such relationship." (84) These immigrants have to construct a sense of community, culture and nation(ality) in a country where they see themselves as different. They have to define both their historical legacies and their present geographic and social realities.

Ashoke and Ashima celebrated all the Bengali festivals and observed all religious rituals and rites with the ethnic community. When Gogol was sixth months old, they invited all of them for *Annaprasan* ceremony, the rice ceremony. Ashoke wore a transparent white Punjabi top over belle-bottom trousers and Ashima wore a silvery saree. The first generation diaspora's adjustments and changes are expedient. They accommodate and adjust to create space and identity in a foreign country. The sense of uprootedness is disturbing to them, more so in the case of new immigrants. They seek advice and suggestion from the ethnic group. "The wives, homesick and bewildered, turned to Ashima for recipe and advice, and she tells them about the carp that is sold in Chinatown, that it is possible to make halwa from cream of wheat. The families drop by one another's home on Sunday afternoons. They argue riotously over the films of Ritwik Ghatak versus those of Satyajit Ray. The CPIM versus the Congress party, North Calcutta versus South Calcutta. For hours they argue about the politics of America, a country in which none of them have right to vote." (38)

But for the second generation diaspora, Gogol and Sonia, identity and problem are rather different, for they have a sense of pride and affinity to India, but it is America that is perceived as 'home.' In America they are born and educated. In America they want to be accepted on their own terms. It is here that they face a sense of alienation in the sense of 'insider' 'outsider.' On one of the fieldtrips in school, Gogol and his classmates are assigned a project 'to rub the surfaces of the gravestones and find out the name of the dead person.' The feeling of alienation and aloofness was doubly intensified because Gogol was old enough to know that there is no Ganguly there. "He was old enough to know that he himself would be burned, not buried, that his body will occupy no plot of earth, that no stone in this country will bear his name beyond life." (69)

The first generation diaspora want to retain their homeland culture and transfer it to the second generation, it is through the eyes of the older generation that the younger generation perceives and learns about homeland culture. Ashoke and Ashima sent Gogol to Bengali classes and culture classes every other Saturday, held in the home of one of their Bengali friends. Though they do face some conflict with their children in this endeavour but the older generation makes certain compromises to maintain inter-generational relation. Ashoke and Ashima learnt to celebrate some of the main festivities of the dominant culture. "For the sake of Gogol and Sonia they celebrated with progressively increasing fanfare, the birth of Christ, an event the children look forward far more than the worship of Durga and Saraswati." (64) Ashoke and Ashima adjusted with food habits of Gogol and Sonia. It is Bengali food that Ashima and Ashoke relished and preferred but for Gogol and Sonia she conceded and made an American dinner once a week as a treat "Shake'n Bake chicken or hamburger helper prepared with ground lamb." (65) Ashoke and Ashima gave in in many ways but it was only to peripheral values i.e. food, dress which were negotiable but not the core values such as their cultural and religious traditions. In fact, the first generation maintain a tangible link with the homeland by continuing tradition as an outward manifestation of their cultural tradition.

Ashoke and Ashima's reaction towards Gogol's friendship with a young girl Ruth is typical of all first generation diaspora. They disapprove and reject all such relationship. It is one accomplishment in Gogol's life about which Ashoke and Ashima are "not in the least bit proud or pleased." They tell him: "you are too young to get involved this way." (117)

Cultural displacement involves the loss of language, family ties and support, and is generally viewed by diasporic groups negatively. In the first generation diaspora, memory and nostalgia play an important role. They cherish and retain all the memories of their homeland and wait very anxiously for the moment of their visit to the country. Their ease and comfort with their own culture can be perceived in their behaviour. In one of the visits to India, Ashoke and Ashima's changed attitude is keenly observed by Gogol and Sonia "Within minutes before their eyes Ashoke and Ashima slip into bolder, less complicated versions of themselves, their voices louder, their smiles wider, revealing a confidence Gogol and Sonia never see on Pamberton Road." (81) In contrast, the second generation, the memories of Calcutta trip is wiped out from their mind "like clothes worn for a special occasion, or for a season that has passed, suddenly cumbersome, irrelevant to their lives." (88) In spite of their attachment to America and American ways they could not be one of them. They are Americans, but different.

Identity for the youngsters is much more complicated, for at the two levels, of private and public, there is dichotomy. Indian values and culture define identity at home, while outside, they are Americans but different. The generation gap is doubly problematic for them, for not only do they face the problems common to many teenagers in relationship to their parents but they also have the problem of the perceived 'Indianness.' The parents expect them to behave in an ideal manner and as most of them have migrated because of betterment in economic or academic field, they expect their children also to perform well academically and professionally. Ashoke and Ashima wanted Gogol to pursue engineering and Moushumi's parents wanted her to be a chemist. In this regard, Prashad comments: "In the US, desi sunders the world into two, the outside world, the world of the workplace, is a world of capital that must be exploited as much as possible, and the inside world, the world of home, is a world of culture that must be protected and cherished . . . whereas morality is protected by the desi migrant within the world of home and culture, immorality is virtually sanctioned in the world of capital."[2] Contrary to this, the second-generation youngsters wanted to choose and adopt a career and a profession of their own liking. Gogol becomes an architect, Moushumi pursued a double major in French. Immersing herself in a third language, a third culture, Sonia becomes a para-lawyer. They feel attracted and have an appreciation for the host culture. Gogol's shifting to live with Maxine's family, adopting and accepting her lifestyle, assimilating their cultural values point towards the second generation's desire of adaptation to the host culture. The first generation parents restrict and refrain such kind of involvement. They want to follow their own cultural values in these matters. As the younger generation could not understand this double standard, they, many a time, grow rebellious in nature. They hide their social relation to avoid confrontation. Gogol did not disclose his relationship with Maxine as long as possible and so did Sonia and Moushumi. It is ironical that Moushumi marries Gogol against her determination not to marry an Indian. Gogol's decision to change his name to Nikhil is also a way to reject his past, though he regrets it when the truth is out.

Jhumpa Lahiri has, thus, very successfully delineated the poetics of exile. The exile has to deal with the two centres, external colonial or modernist and the internal or national filtering into a personal identity. The chief feature of the poetic of exile is the trial during which it deals with these centers, sometimes rejecting and sometimes accepting them. Lahiri has deftly narrated the struggle of these immigrants to assimilate and adapt the host culture and in the process of alteration they give up the rigid hold of their past and alternate his/her behaviour with the need of situation. Ashoke and Ashima's acceptance of Maxine in his son's life, Ashima's consent for Sonia's marriage to Ben, a half Jewish and half Chinese boy, all indicate their changed perspective. The death of Ashoke brings a change in the life of Sonia and Gogol also, the second generation. Now they can experience the trauma and pain their parents have undergone during the death of their parents. Now they can share the agony and pain their parents felt for being far away from their home. At the end of the novel, Ashima's decision to live six months in Calcutta, in India and six months in America with Gogol and Sonia make her realize that she belongs nowhere and at the same time everywhere "True to the meaning of her name, she is without border, without a home of her own, a resident everywhere and nowhere." (276), and so with Gogol who is an alien both in India and America.

NOTES

1. Jhumpa Lahiri, *The Namesake* (Harper Collins India, 2004).
2. V. Prashad, *The Karma of Brown Folks* (Minneapolis: University of Minnestoa Press, 2000), p. 14.